PLAYFUL DESIGN
CREATING GAME EXPERIENCES IN EVERYDAY INTERFACES

John Ferrara

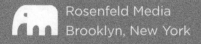

Rosenfeld Media
Brooklyn, New York

Playful Design: Creating Game Experiences in Everyday Interfaces
By John Ferrara

Rosenfeld Media, LLC

457 Third Street, #4R

Brooklyn, New York

11215 USA

On the Web: www.rosenfeldmedia.com

Please send errors to: errata@rosenfeldmedia.com

Publisher: Louis Rosenfeld

Developmental Editor: JoAnn Simony

Copyeditor: Stephanie Hiebert

Interior Layout Tech: Danielle Foster

Cover Design: The Heads of State

Indexer: Nancy Guenther

Proofreader: Ben Tedoff

ISBN: 1-933820-14-4

ISBN-13: 978-1-933820-14-9

LCCN: 2012935786

Printed and bound in the United States of America

DEDICATION

This book is dedicated to Amanda,
who has given me more than I can ever repay

And to Margot, who has been my greatest inspiration

HOW TO USE THIS BOOK

Who Should Read This Book?

Playful Design is primarily written for designers of conventional software, websites, mobile apps, and other computer-mediated user experiences who are looking for novel approaches to creating compelling, satisfying, and enjoyable designs. It's well suited to anyone who specializes in human-computer interaction, digital product strategy, interaction design, information architecture, usability engineering, graphic design, application development, or similar roles.

This book also is intended to be accessible to a broader audience of readers who aren't user experience (UX) practitioners, but who want to learn more about how games can achieve great things in the real world. If this sounds like you, then you might like to start by skipping ahead to Part III, where I survey a variety of case studies, before circling back to the beginning of the book.

Game designers will find new ways to think about the impact they can have on the world. Though much of the content in this book reviews practices and design patterns with which you're probably very familiar (especially in Part II), I hope that the overall picture I draw will lead to fresh insights into your work. I also invite you to explore how opening a relationship with the UX design community can broaden the reach of games.

I do not assume that readers have a ton of experience playing video games, although I believe you need to play a pretty good amount to design well for them. It's okay if you're not the world's biggest gamer, but maybe you can be persuaded to get into what I believe is a very worthwhile use of your time.

If you do play games, then I think you're going to have a lot of fun with this book. You can consider the countless hours you've spent playing them to have been study sessions, as all of your experience will help you to get more out of every single chapter. You're well prepared to reflect on the design of games and their broader significance in everyday life.

What's in This Book?

This book is a call to action for UX designers to incorporate game design into their toolkit, and a guide for how to apply it most effectively.

The **Introduction** offers my perspective on recent fads in the application of game design, and an explanation of why I believe they have been fundamentally flawed.

Part I: Playful Thinking

Chapter 1: Why We Should Care about Games makes a case for taking games seriously as a form of human-computer interaction, and explains the reasons UX designers in particular should take an active interest in them.

Chapter 2: Understanding Games provides a basic theoretical background on games, defining their primary characteristics and exploring their relationship to everyday life.

Chapter 3: The Elements of Player Experience presents a model for thinking about player experiences that draws on an established UX model. This chapter is intended to provide a basis for thinking through the design choices that make games challenging, satisfying, and enjoyable.

Chapter 4: Player Motivations reviews some of the most common reasons why people feel motivated to play games.

Part II: Designing Game Experiences

Chapter 5: Ten Tips for Building a Better Game is a list of things that you can do to improve your chances of creating a successful design. If you're starting a game project right now and need a quick guide before jumping in, this chapter is a good place to begin.

Chapter 6: Developing a Game Concept lays out some of the key decision points that you should think through when coming up with a vision for a game.

Chapter 7: Creating Game Prototypes describes methods for quickly mocking up prototypes that will save time and money in the design and development of a game.

Chapter 8: Playtesting explains how to evaluate a game with players and get actionable insights for design.

Chapter 9: Behavioral Tools discusses elements of design that can encourage players to adopt certain behaviors in a game and give shape to the experience.

Chapter 10: Rewards in Games lists some of the most common reward systems employed in games, and provides best practices for their design.

What Comes with This Book

This book's companion website (rosenfeldmedia.com/books/game-design) contains more information about how to incorporate game design principles into your user experience design practice. You can also find a calendar of my workshops and presentations, and a place to engage others in conversation. The book's diagrams and other illustrations are available (when possible, under a Creative Commons license) for you to download and include in your own presentations. You can find these on Flickr at www.flickr.com/photos/rosenfeldmedia/sets/.

FREQUENTLY ASKED QUESTIONS

What do you mean when you refer to "video games"?

Throughout this book, I use the phrase "video games" to refer to computer-mediated games of all types, from *World of Warcraft* to *Words with Friends*. This may be a more general usage than a purist would select, but I use it because it's a conventional and recognizable way to distinguish this subtype of games from other forms. I use the term "games" to refer to the broader class of experiences that includes video games as well as board games, sports, card games, gambling, and so on. A more robust discussion of what it means for something to be a game or a video game is found in Chapter 2. See page 16.

Are you suggesting that UX designers should become game designers?

I'm proposing that UX designers adopt game design as a competency that they can enlist, alongside our existing competencies, to solve real problems. I argue that, to do this effectively, it is critical for us to acquire the theory, skills, and processes that will allow us to build truly rewarding game experiences. This book is intended to lay the groundwork for UX practitioners to begin developing this capability in earnest. So, no, I'm not suggesting that we should rethink our careers, but rather that we should grow within them. For more about why we should, see Chapter 1.

Are video games really that important?

This depends on what they're doing, but they absolutely can be. Today, video games are being designed that forge connections between people, teach subjects in schools, encourage healthier living, support charitable giving, fight world hunger, and promote the cause of peace. I believe that games are up to these tasks and can offer fresh approaches to making the world a better place. See Chapters 11–13 to read more about such real-world examples.

More generally, I would argue that play is an essential part of living. It's the process by which great discoveries are made, industries are built, and people fall in love. The instinctive human drive toward play continuously pushes us to find new ways to understand and influence the world around us.

Isn't this just another way to say that we should try to make things more fun to use?

Designers can't just set about designing fun, for at least two reasons. First, it's a very subjective and cultural quality, carrying a lot of different meanings for a lot of different people. The type of fun you might engineer for one person might be boring, irritating, or offensive to many others. Second, fun is an effect of a well-designed game, rather than something that can be molded directly out of clay. So it's better to focus on creating a high-quality player experience and allow fun to emerge from the player's interaction with it. I talk more about the motivations that drive people to play games in Chapter 4. See page 36.

Apart from fun, games also have a lot of other positive effects that shouldn't be overlooked. UX designers will find great value in exploring how they can make life more intuitive, more engaging, more memorable, more meaningful, more rewarding, more productive, more effective, and more successful.

Are you saying that everything people do should be turned into a game?

No. In this book I show how UX designers can find great opportunity in building on the innate gamefulness residing in everyday experiences to create better ways for people to interact with computers than would otherwise be available. However, this approach is not appropriate in every situation, and pursuing game strategies where there is no game to be found will result in projects that are doomed to failure. For an explanation of such pitfalls, I encourage you to read the Introduction. See page xv.

But I also believe that it's simply a good idea for UX designers to have a sense of what's going on in games, because other kinds of benefits can be drawn from them that are relevant to our profession. Many games have amazing user interfaces, which can be a great source of inspiration in our own work. Whether it's discovering new design patterns or getting a fresh perspective on mediated collaboration, there's much to learn from the great design work being done in games. So the message of this book is certainly not "turn everything into a game."

How can I get involved with the best communities that are doing work in this area?

There are a few conferences I recommend attending. Each year the Game Developers Conference (San Francisco, GDconf.com) hosts a rotating set of smaller summits dedicated to games in real-world contexts, and the general conference is a great opportunity to learn practices and methods of the established game design industry. More specialized conferences include Games for Health (Boston, GamesForHealth.org), dedicated to games that improve wellness and healthcare; Games for Change (New York City, GamesForChange.org), which showcases games that promote social causes; and Games, Learning and Society (Madison, Wisconsin, GLSconference.org), which is largely devoted to educational games. I would love to see substantial numbers of UX designers attend these conferences. All of these groups also have very active e-mail discussion communities, which you can join on their websites. Finally, I would encourage you to find a local chapter of the International Game Developers' Association (IGDA.org) and attend their meanings to learn, connect, and even introduce a UX perspective.

CONTENTS

FOREWORD

 The word "game" conjures up numerous meanings for people. We think of fun, of playing, of winning and losing; we think of competition. But we often miss the depth of discovery and reward that games provide. We don't always recognize the high level of cognitive functionality that games can bring to the table. And, before this book, most of us haven't paid attention to the variety of environments in which games can work serious mojo.

In this age of explosive information and the inevitable rise in architecting that information, John Ferrara's theory that game design should be combined with user experience is not only creative but prescient. We're seeing games move toward a social crescendo in so many areas—health, education, innovation, scenario planning—that the opportunity for the UX community is enormous. If a fundamental goal of user experience is to elevate human-computer interaction, what better way to up-level that interaction than by infusing games? Because make no mistake: games have a long and profound relationship with human beings. They appeal to our fundamental need to surprise and be surprised, to learn and teach, to discover and connect, to analyze and intuit.

But to echo the author's perspective, it behooves UX designers to distinguish between trendy gamification—really all lipstick and no sex—and robust, compelling game design that ignites our systems of pleasure. Points and "Likes" are a decent first step, but feedback loops and small, surmountable obstacles are better. Make the user experience "seductive" (to borrow an expression from Kathy Sierra). Design it so it talks to and tickles human psychology. Think of the value intrinsic in a worthwhile transaction and leverage what lies beneath. *That's* where your design can inspire loyalty, evangelism, and excitement. That's where you can create an "epic win" for everyone.

The UX field has made ongoing and significant improvements in the way users navigate online space, and it's only a matter of time before it starts to show a prowess in game space. What an exciting time for all of us! So go forth, apply the knowledge of game design John offers, and play with all your might.

—Sunni Brown
Expert meeting gamer and coauthor of *Gamestorming*

INTRODUCTION

Messification

When it started, I have to admit that I was really excited.

As I was in the process of writing this book, out of pure coincidence interest in the positive effects that video games can have in the real world spontaneously erupted within the general culture. Although this was an idea that a lot of people had been promoting for some time, it had mostly flown under the public's radar. Back in 2008, I had been a little worried that a UX book about solving real-world problems through games would be seen as a bit fringe. So when interest started to gather entirely of its own accord, I thought it was a great thing.

Then it started getting scary.

Things labeled "games" are springing up everywhere, and many them can be seen as games in only the most superficial ways. The pervasive problem with these implementations has been that they are designed with insufficient regard for the quality of the player experience. They contain none of the joy, fascination, and complexity that makes games the beautiful interactions they are. In the worst cases, they demonstrate an impoverished, cynical, and exploitative view of games and the innate human drive to engage in play.

Take, for example, the *McNuggets Saucy Challenge*, a Flash game on McDonald's public website. The challenge in question is to dip your McNugget into six different sauces mirroring a pattern that increments by one sauce for every successful cycle (like Simon). When your memory inevitably falters, you're invited to post your score—with McAdvertising—to Facebook as a prerequisite to being ranked on a leaderboard. This design is impoverished because it doesn't offer meaningful play. It is cynical because it shows no regard for the legitimacy of play as a human endeavor. It is exploitative because it pursues self-serving ends that are disproportionate to the value of the gameplay experience it offers in return. I wish I could say that this example is an exception, but today it's much closer to being the norm.

Then, a graceless and overly memorable buzzword crashed into the culture: *gamification*. The name itself betrays the conceptual flaw of this fad, implying an experience that is by its nature something other than a game but dressed up to resemble one. And indeed, many implementations that fall under the "gamification" banner amount to little more than points and leaderboards tacked onto an underlying system that remains otherwise unchanged. These kinds of approaches will not survive, because they do not value gameplay, so players will not value them.

Making matters worse, "gamification" also has a troublingly imprecise definition that seems to vary by the person using it. It has been applied to any game that attempts to achieve something beyond its virtual margins. It is terribly misleading to use the same word to describe the successful work being done by designers like Ian Bogost, Scot Osterweil, and Jane McGonigal and to describe the McNuggets game and similar follies. As the reach of the inevitable backlash grows, a mounting cultural skepticism of gamification threatens to stifle other, innovative applications of game design.

It's all turned into a big mess.

This ballooning enthusiasm around games closely mirrors Gartner's "hype cycle," which describes the typical pattern of adoption for a new technology (Figure 0.1).[1] After initially arriving on the scene, a new technology's visibility increases quickly until it reaches the peak of inflated expectations—where people rush to the technology without a realistic strategy for putting it to its most effective use. Then a preponderance of early adopters discover that, surprise surprise, the technology doesn't deliver what they thought it would, and the hype collapses into the trough of disillusionment. As of early 2012, I believe that the hype cycle for games has crested and is plunging headlong toward this low point.

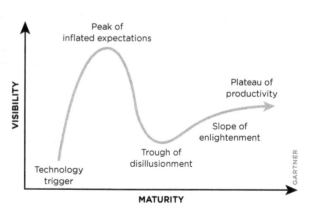

FIGURE 0.1
Following the typical path of the Gartner hype cycle, in early 2012 gamification was somewhere just past the peak of inflated expectations.

1 Gartner Research, "Research Methodologies: Hype Cycles," www.gartner.com/technology/research/methodologies/hype-cycle.jsp.

The good news is that after bottoming out, the cycle turns upward again. People start to discover and embrace best practices for using the technology, more success stories start to emerge, and the technology eventually finds productive mainstream adoption. With this book, I hope to start moving toward a post-hype discussion of how games can most effectively achieve great things in the real world.

If there's one message I would like to convey through this book, it is that designers who are creating games must be centrally concerned with the quality of the player experience. This is, after all, the reason why people invest their time in games in the first place. It's important to realize that there's an innate selfishness to gameplay. People don't play games out of loyalty to your brand or because they want to solve world hunger. They play because they value the experience. Trading off enjoyable gameplay in service of external objectives is always self-defeating.

To create high-quality player experiences, UX designers must develop a fundamental competency with game design. The largest part of this book, then, is dedicated to the theory, skills, and practices that will lead practitioners to more successful outcomes.

CHAPTER 1

Why We Should Care about Games

This puzzle is killing me. I've looked at the chain from 20 different angles, and I just can't see the solution. I decide to take a stab in the dark and twist one of the blue pieces inward. It costs me 300 points. Crap. Then it hits me: if I bend the whole chain into thirds, all of the orange pieces will be on the inside, just where they're supposed to be. That does the trick. I finish the puzzle and I'm off to the next level.

I'm playing *Foldit* on my home computer. Its look and feel is as familiar as that of any video game (that is, any game mediated by a computer), with its bloops and bleeps and multicolored flying sparkles. But the puzzle itself is actually modeled on an object from nature: a protein chain that must be folded into a particular shape (Figure 1.1). This is a complex challenge in modern biochemistry, and even supercomputers aren't especially good at finding the solutions. But people's natural aptitudes for spatial manipulation and creative thinking make them better suited to the task. "Without a human being to help out, a computer just kind of flails about trying to get the pieces to fit together,"[1] explains Seth Cooper, one of the designers of *Foldit*. He's part of a team of computer scientists and biochemists at the University of Washington who collaborated to build *Foldit* as a way to make the task fun, engaging, and accessible to the general public.

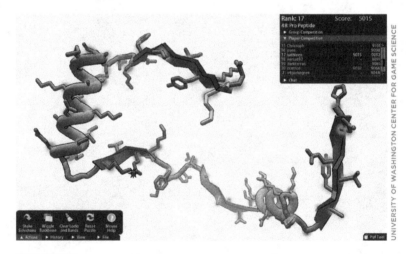

FIGURE 1.1

In *Foldit*, players solve puzzles based on real proteins.

You might recall that *Foldit* hit the news in September 2011 after its research team published the structure of a protein related to the growth of a virus that causes AIDS in monkeys—a solution that had eluded researchers for over a

---

1 Phone interview with the author, March 8, 2010.

decade.[2] When the problem was put to *Foldit* players, they solved it in just 10 days. For the most part these are not trained scientists, but people who just play the game because they enjoy the challenge it presents. Given a discovery of sufficient magnitude, it's conceivable that anyone playing this video game— even with no prior knowledge of biochemistry—could win a Nobel Prize.

As a user experience (UX) designer, I can't help but think that an example such as this, in which a designer took a problem that we would normally handle through conventional software and instead successfully approached it through a video game, is something really worth our attention.

An Expanding Role

Today there are many experiences that, like *Foldit*, reach beyond the traditional role video games have occupied. There are games that serve as social glue between old friends, and games that bring strangers together to collaborate. There are games that help people meet their life objectives, and games that let people reward others for meeting theirs. There are games that facilitate creative self-expression, that help people understand the news, that train doctors to save lives, that advocate for human rights, and that work to engage people in politics. I would say that designers are pushing the boundaries of what it means to be a game, except that few boundaries now seem to exist.

Video game design and UX design share some common traits, and as games spread out into new realms where they create real benefits for individuals, families, schools, governments, businesses, and societies, the distinction between our disciplines will become fuzzier and less important. This is a great thing, because it exposes a space into which UX design can expand and gain access to entirely new ways of enabling more compelling, inventive, and enjoyable experiences. In this book I advocate that, as designers of conventional software and Web user experiences, we should incorporate video game design into our tool kit and learn how to appropriately apply game solutions to real problems of design. As I'll show, we have everything to gain.

Why Do Games Matter?

There is a strong cultural bias that games must necessarily be frivolous. When people say that something is "just a game," they mean it would be a mistake to take it seriously. When they warn that something is "not a game," they mean it should be treated with the proper gravity. So why should UX professionals, who design serious applications, take games seriously?

In fact, there are tangible reasons why it would be a serious mistake not to.

---

2   Khatib, F., DiMaio, F., Foldit Contenders Group, Foldit Void Crushers Group, Cooper, S., Kazmierczyk, M.,... Baker, D. (2011). Crystal structure of a monomeric retroviral protease solved by protein folding game players. *Nature Structural & Molecular Biology*, 18, 1175–1177. Note: This is by far the longest and stodgiest citation in the book. I promise.

Games Can Solve Real Problems

Above all things, games must be enjoyable. But that shouldn't be taken to mean that they must necessarily serve frivolous ends. The fact that many familiar video games are pure entertainment is a matter of convention, not of necessity.

It's not hard to find games that have effects in the real world. Gambling is one example. Most people would accept that poker, blackjack, and craps fit conventional definitions of games. Modern slot machines are, in every way, video games. But these games also have real impacts on players. They can be ruinous to those who develop compulsive gambling habits, and when that happens, to say "It's just a game" has no real meaning.

Conversely, games can be directed toward positive ends. For example, there's a rapidly growing sector of video games designed to improve people's health. Exergames like *Wii Fit* and *Just Dance* build physical activity right into the gameplay and have proven to be massively popular among players. The annual Games for Health conference is dedicated to exploring ways that games can be used in physical therapy, health education, and disease management. Other designers have used video games to encourage charitable giving, build communities, increase awareness of social issues, educate students, and increase the fuel efficiency of cars. (I'll return to each of these later in the book.)

This is the single greatest reason why we should care about video games: they have the capacity to solve real problems in the real world. Moreover, given the right circumstances (discussed in Chapter 2), they can do so more effectively than nongame user interfaces applied to the same problems. The cultural bias that games are necessarily frivolous only holds us back from exploiting a deep mode of interactivity. To take greatest advantage of the capabilities that game design can bring to our tool kit, we need to throw that prejudice into the trash.

Overlap between Disciplines Creates Learning Opportunities

User experience design and video game design are something like siblings who were raised in separate homes. It's easy to understand both as forms of human-computer interaction and as centrally concerned with the design of experience. But UX design creates experiences that help people meet their real-world needs, whereas game design is about the experience for the sake of the experience.

Although related, these disciplines diverged in the 1960s and '70s when some software developers chose to pursue productivity applications and others chose to produce entertainment. Both camps grew into massive industries, developing their own methods, best practices, design patterns, gurus, and killer apps. Since we matured largely in professional isolation, today there is a great opportunity for us to learn from one another. Both UX designers and game designers can benefit from discovering the solutions that each has independently developed for similar problems. In the near future, I have every expectation that these disciplines will continue to merge, overlap, and become harder to delineate (Figure 1.2).

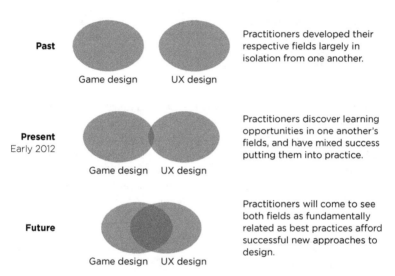

FIGURE 1.2
As time goes on and practitioners find more value in one another's fields, UX design and game design will become intertwined.

Games Are Vastly Popular

Popularity may be a crude measure of merit, but the pronounced success of the video game industry makes it impossible to ignore. The numbers speak to a cultural change under way, where gaming is becoming a part of everyday life.

Sales Data

Consumers are collectively spending huge amounts of money on video games, which are emerging as both an important sector of the global economy and a dominant form of recreation.

- The video game industry saw total worldwide revenue of $24 billion in 2010.[3] More Americans now play video games (63 percent) than go out to the movies (53 percent).[4] People's habits are shifting away from traditional media, with video games occupying a larger proportion of our downtime.

- In November 2011, *Call of Duty: Modern Warfare 3* took in more than $775 million worldwide in five days, making it the highest-grossing launch of any form of entertainment in history.[5] The title was actually just the latest in a succession of games to have claimed the same record, and video games now appear unbeatable by other media in terms of pure sales.

- Guinness lists Microsoft's Kinect controller for the Xbox as the fastest-selling consumer electronics device in history, with 8 million units sold in its first 60 days on the market.[6]

Demographic Data

Video games were once very much a niche entertainment, played mostly by young boys on home consoles. That's no longer the case. The video game industry has grown by branching out aggressively into other demographics, publishing titles with wide-ranging appeal and putting them on systems that are easier to use (and often already in your pocket). Today, video games are enjoyed by a very diverse set of consumers, and there is no longer a single profile for the typical game player (Figure 1.3).

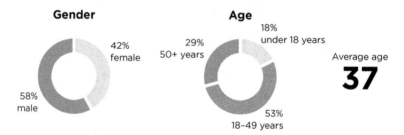

FIGURE 1.3
Demographic profiles of US video game players as of 2011, according to survey data from the Entertainment Software Association.

3 NPD Group. (2011, March). *Games industry: Total consumer spend (2010).* Referenced at www.npd.com/press/releases/press_110113.html.

4 NPD Group. (2009, May). *More Americans play video games than go out to the movies.* Retrieved from www.npd.com/wps/portal/npd/us/news/pressreleases/pr_090520.

5 Activision press release. (2011, November 17). Retrieved from investor.activision.com/releasedetail.cfm?ReleaseID=624766.

6 *Guinness world records 2011: Gamer's edition.* (2011). Brady Games.

- Of all US video game players, 58 percent are male and 42 percent are female. Women 18 and older now actually represent a larger segment of all video game players than do boys 17 and younger.[7]

- The average age of US video game players is 37. One reason for that relatively high number is that people who grew up playing video games never really stopped. Fifty-three percent of all players are between 18 and 49 years old, and 29 percent are over 50.[8]

- Social games like *FarmVille* in particular have found a home among more mature people and among women. A 2010 survey found that 93 percent of social game players in the United States and the United Kingdom are over 21, with an average age of 43; and 55 percent are female.[9]

I could go on. But the real significance of these numbers lies in the effect that video games, with this level of popularity, are having on culture and society.

Cultural and Social Change

Particularly significant for UX designers, video games are becoming a normal way of interacting with machines. On average, people who play games in the United States spend 13 hours per week with them, and in extreme (but not uncommon) cases, more than 40 hours per week.[10] A 2008 survey found that fully 97 percent of American kids between the ages of 12 and 17 played video games.[11] Among younger age groups, gaming is a ubiquitous activity that will inevitably influence the way they think about interactive experiences. Those of us who work in the UX field want to leverage the conventions with which people have grown most familiar. UX designers need to understand games out of necessity, just to stay current.

Video games are also building and shaping social relationships among people. For example, *World of Warcraft* allows players to form guilds with one another to pool resources and take on challenges collectively. Guilds facilitate a social experience that has resulted in friendships, rivalries, and even marriages among people who have no connection outside of the game

---

7 Entertainment Software Association. *Essential facts about the computer and video game industry: 2011 sales, demographic and usage data.* Retrieved from www.theesa.com/facts/pdfs/ESA_EF_2011.pdf.

8 Ibid.

9 Information Solutions Group. *2010 social gaming research.* Retrieved from www.infosolutionsgroup.com/2010_PopCap_Social_Gaming_Research_Results.pdf.

10 NPD Group. (2010, May 27). *Extreme gamers spend two full days per week playing video games.* Retrieved from www.npd.com/wps/portal/npd/us/news/pressreleases/pr_100527b.

11 Lenhart, A., Kahne, J., Middaugh, E., Macgill, A., Evans, C., & Vitak, J. (2008, September 16). *Teens, video games, and civics.* Pew Internet & American Life Project. Retrieved from www.pewinternet.org/Reports/2008/Teens-Video-Games-and-Civics.aspx.

universe.[12] Other games, such as *CityVille*, are created expressly to serve social ends, and they give players little choice but to involve as many friends as possible in the game experience in order to advance (Figure 1.4).

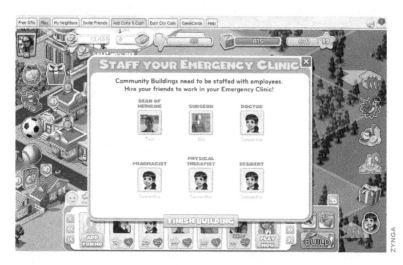

FIGURE 1.4
CityVille promotes a social experience by giving advantages to players who work together to progress in the game.

All of these games comprise entirely new ways for people to relate to one another through a shared experience in a separate universe driven by communal goals. As video games continue to gain in popularity and the generation growing up inside these virtual environments matures, we can be sure that the implications for society as a whole will be far-reaching— even if it's not yet entirely clear what they will be.

As an inevitable consequence of their popularity, video games are gaining a new cultural legitimacy that's elevating them to a central place in our shared consciousness. Emerging from a cultural backwater, video games have entered the mainstream in a big way.

Games Drive Innovation

Game design has built up a sea of creative thinking that runs both deep and wide. The fierce competition among modern game companies has forced them to innovate, and one way they try to differentiate themselves from

---

12 Rushkoff, D., & Dretzin, R. (Writers); Dretzin, R. (Director). (2010, February 2). Digital nation: Live on the virtual frontier [Television series episode]. In Fanning, D. (Executive producer), *Frontline*. Arlington, VA: PBS. Retrieved from www.pbs.org/wgbh/pages/frontline/digitalnation.

one another is through interface design. Increasingly, game makers are experimenting with technologies like motion control, gestural interfaces, and linked displays (I discuss these in greater depth in Chapter 14). These will drive the development of inexpensive, high-quality consumer products that can be repurposed for applications well beyond gaming. If we're not paying attention to games, then we're missing out on some of the most exciting innovations in UX design.

The modern sophistication of computers and consumer electronics owes a lot to video games, which created a demand for devices that had faster processors, richer graphical displays, sophisticated sound, and intuitive means of input.[13] Games also predispose people to user interfaces that make the interaction feel like play. It's easy to forget how much fun the original Macintosh was to use in 1984, but that was a big factor in its appeal. Today we get that same toylike feeling when we pick up an iPad.

Why Us?

I believe that UX designers' core competencies predispose us to acquiring the methods and practices that lead to the design of high-quality player experiences. Even better, we can bring a unique perspective to game design that can give rise to fresh approaches. In particular, certain specific attributes of the UX community suit effective game design.

- **We've got experience in experience.** Our practice is built entirely around elevating the user's qualitative experience of a design. User-centered design is closely related to the player-centric thinking that's common to all good game experiences.

- **Games are moving toward our areas of expertise.** For those of us who have worked in the development of online systems (especially social and mobile applications), game design has arrived in our backyard. The collision between games and the Internet has opened new creative avenues for designers. Our aptitudes in these realms can bring new thinking to game design, just as demand is ramping up.

- **We know how to work the technology.** We design experiences using software technology as our raw material. Video games arise from many of the same root technologies that we use to design software, and they're often played on the same devices. The skills we've developed working on these platforms translate well to games.

- **We're in touch with real-world problems.** Businesses and public and private agencies are increasingly putting up funds for games that

---

13 Thompson, C. (2010, December 31). The influence of gaming [Radio interview]. In *On the Media*. New York, NY: WNYC. Retrieved from www.onthemedia.org/2010/dec/31/the-influence-of-gaming.

solve real-world problems. People working in the game design industry tend to be more focused on creating unique intellectual properties in service of pure consumer models, leaving a gap that creates a demand for skilled designers. With our established backgrounds developing products for diverse clients and projects, UX designers are well positioned to fill that gap.

One Note of Caution

I want to be careful to say that I'm not suggesting the UX design community is *presently* ready to just sit down and start making games. Game design is a robust and cerebral practice in its own right, and much of it turns our usual ways of thinking upside down. Operating successfully in the games domain means learning an entirely new set of competencies and gaining experience putting them into practice. This book is intended to get you started down that road.

How Can Games Benefit Us?

Let's suppose we accept that video games are important and that UX designers should be paying attention to them. How, then, do we actually make use of any new knowledge or skills we gain from deepening our understanding of game design? I can think of three ways that we can incorporate game design into our work.

By Reenvisioning Conventional Experiences as Games

Call this the direct method. Some everyday tasks can be redefined to be experienced as games. Users become players, following the rules and seeking the objectives set by the designers, and the game in and of itself is their motivation to engage in the experience. Many applications naturally lend themselves to such treatment, as I'll discuss in Chapter 2.

This approach resembles a current fad that some people call "gamification." I'm not a fan of the term, because it implies that the designed product remains fundamentally an application that just happens to have some game elements tacked on. Such an approach can lead to half measures that are transparently dressed up to obscure the application at its root. Instead, I'm talking about reconceiving applications first and foremost as true games that are enjoyed for their game-ness, but that also happen to have effects in the real world.

This approach requires a conceptual leap on our part to picture how everyday activities could succeed as games. Part III of this book explores some ways that inventive people have accomplished this.

Jesse Schell

I think the recent enthusiasm for "gamification" is a result of a much larger and more important trend. Gradually, ever so gradually, the nature of design has been changing. While design used to be all about efficiency and effectiveness, it has more and more become focused on pleasure. It is a shift from work to play, from duty to enjoyment, from spartan discipline to living in the moment. It's as if the whole world has woken up and said, "Hey…what if we just made everything more…enjoyable?"

And naturally, the world is turning to the game designers. Game design is different from traditional design, in that games have no purpose other than to create pleasure. And the world has realized that, if we are to make everything more pleasurable, the game designers may have some knowledge that is special and useful. But applying this knowledge wisely and well does not always mean turning everything into a game. What it means is attaining a deeper understanding of the nature of human pleasure, and finding ways to strengthen and enhance the natural pleasures that are part of all kinds of human activity. The key is to understand that games are fun and engaging not because they are games, but because they were created by people who understand the nature of what people find pleasurable.

Jesse Schell is an associate professor of entertainment technology at Carnegie Mellon University, and CEO of Schell Games. His book The Art of Game Design *is among the most influential texts on the subject.*

By Drawing Inspiration from Games

Of course, not everything can be redefined as a game. Trying to force a game structure onto an application that's just not suited to it won't work, and I wouldn't argue that you should try. But with the conventions of games becoming a familiar way for people to interact with machines, you can instead realize tremendous benefit from incorporating conventions and design patterns that are familiar to people from their interactions with games.

One of the most dramatic examples of this indirect approach is *Second Life*, which is at its heart a communications system akin to a chat room that lacks the objective-driven play of a true game. But *Second Life* adopts the convention of physical presence in games to transform the experience into something much richer (Figure 1.5).

FIGURE 1.5
Second Life is not a game, but it builds a rich interactive experience by adopting the conventions of games.

However, not all indirect approaches need to adopt a game skin so thoroughly. Just being tuned in to the ways that games operate can inspire new insights and creative solutions to everyday problems of design.

By Just Making Games

One last way that we could use games is as games. In other words, there's no need to import them into the UX world in order to get something of value from them, because games themselves are valuable experiences. When we sit down to play a video game, we fully engage our consciousness to surmount a difficult challenge. We learn and acquire new skills at a fast pace. We apply strategic thinking, exercise creativity, and seek out the most efficient solutions to problems. We develop and deepen relationships with other people taking part in the play. We enjoy ourselves and then reflect fondly on the experience when it's over.

Why shouldn't these things, in and of themselves, be enough? If our central concern is the quality of an interactive experience, then there's no reason why video games, which can satisfy people so richly, should be excluded. Interactions with software or websites can often be aimless and arbitrary anyway, without the clearly defined objectives we like to assume in their design. When no such goals exist, people can find much more meaning in solving a puzzle, outfoxing a friend, or building a virtual home. Our ability to deliver these experiences to people can only deepen the relevance of our field.

Ready, Set,...

Video games present great new opportunities to UX designers, the limits of which are set only by the extent of our own imagination and creativity. At the same time, when we create a game we must take on a new set of responsibilities to our users (who we would need to get used to calling "players") to support experiences that engage, excite, and entertain. Games have an obligation to their players' sense of active enjoyment that goes beyond what UX designers normally need to deliver. That's also precisely the thing that makes game design so interesting. Creating a new class of playful designs that can make life more captivating while also making it more successful is an opportunity that we should savor.

So let's go. This is going to be fun.

CHAPTER 2

Understanding
Games

It's hard to pin down a set of characteristics that is common to all games, because games can vary so broadly in form. Think about the differences in play between and even within these categories of games:

- **Card games:** poker, blackjack, Hearts, solitaire, Killer Bunnies, Yu-Gi-Oh!, Magic: The Gathering

- **Board games:** chess, checkers, backgammon, Clue, Scrabble, Pictionary, Trivial Pursuit, Twister, tic-tac-toe

- **Puzzles:** crosswords, sudoku, Jumble, mazes, matchstick puzzles

- **Gambling:** slot machines, roulette, craps, horse racing, state lotteries, office football pools

- **Sports:** baseball, boxing, triathlon, ice hockey, Olympic ballroom dancing

- **Backyard games:** tag, hide-and-seek, bocce, badminton, tug-of-war

- **Role-playing games:** *Dungeons & Dragons*, *Final Fantasy*, *Mass Effect*, LARPing

- **Music and rhythm games:** *Rock Band*, *Dance Central*, *SingStar*, *PaRappa the Rapper*

- **Action/arcade games:** *Pac-Man*, *Centipede*, *Qix*, *Tetris*, *Angry Birds*, *Geometry Wars*

- **Game shows:** *Jeopardy!*, *The Price Is Right*, *Wheel of Fortune*, *Let's Make a Deal*, *Family Feud*

What properties make all of these things games, and what properties distinguish games from one another? To have a meaningful discussion of games, we first need to get a handle on what they are.

Defining Games

There is no single agreed-upon definition for games, but only frameworks that are of greater or lesser usefulness. This book describes how UX practitioners can make use of games, often in ways that lie outside of their traditional purposes. Toward that end, it's helpful to have a broad and inclusive definition of games.

Using a broad definition is okay because it's what has allowed game designers to continually invent new ways to play. Many games succeed by breaking out of the mold that defined what people had previously thought games could be—from musical-instrument games such as *Rock Band* to the seven-second microgames of *WarioWare*. If designers didn't conceive of games in broad terms, we wouldn't have so many diverse ways to play.

Top-down approaches to defining games tend to be either so specific that it's easy to find exceptions, or so vague that they don't help to inform design.

For those reasons I am staying away from a dictionary-style definition and instead will build from the bottom up by focusing on the shared characteristics of games. I'll start by discussing games in general, and then focus on what makes video games a distinct subtype.

Characteristics of Games in General

Although games can vary widely in form, a small set of basic characteristics is common to all of them. Taken together, they describe the essential mechanic of play for any game, as distinct from any other game. Many other characteristics are common to games, but they are either products of the interactions between these basic characteristics (for example, conflict), or elements of the design that can be modified without changing the underlying mechanic of play (for example, aesthetics). The characteristics described in the sections that follow are what make a game a game.

Objectives

All games have some type of objective, set for the player by the game's creator. An objective can be defined as a specific condition or set of conditions that all of the players are trying either to achieve or to maintain. Games work best when objectives are:

- **Explicit.** Players need to understand what they're working toward (or at least have a reasonable opportunity to figure it out).

- **Measurable.** Players need to have some means of saying whether an objective has actually been met, because any ambiguity puts the validity of the game experience in question. In bowling, a pin has either fallen or it hasn't. Measurability can be something of a problem in games like baseball, which needs trusted umpires to judge things that are difficult to measure.

- **Reliable.** Moving the goalposts goes against people's instinctive sense of fairness. Most of us are sympathetic to the idea that a game's stated objectives should remain the same as players work toward them.

Some game objectives mark the point at which play stops. In Clue, whoever correctly names the character, room, and murder weapon is declared the winner, and at that point the game ends. While it's common to end the game when such an objective is met, it's also not the only possible structure. When people play tag, for example, they just keep meeting the same objective over and over again until no one feels like playing anymore.

Many games contain multiple smaller objectives for players to meet. The top-level objective in Trivial Pursuit is to be the first to reenter the center of the board and correctly answer a trivia question. To do that, players first need to collect each of the six colored chips. To do that, players need to answer a lot of questions correctly as they move around the board. Such minor objectives, which may be required or optional, are helpful in longer games because they give people a feeling of progress and so keep them engaged in the play experience.

In other games the objective is not to meet a condition but to maintain one. In Jenga or Twister, the game goes on as long players can sustain a precarious balance, ending only when everything comes tumbling down. This goal of maintaining a particular condition is a feature of many video games, where a common objective is to keep a character alive. The ultimate objective in *Pac-Man* is to get a high score, but to do that players need to stay alive as long as possible. The game has no winning condition, but rather ends when the player fails.

Environmental Constraints

All games contain elements that place hard limits on what players can and cannot do. These things have physical characteristics that the players are unable to affect without changing the game. The design of these environmental constraints can be a very important element of the game experience, because they have a significant role in giving the gameplay its structural shape.

Environmental constraints include the boundaries and structure of the play space. Chess is played on an 8×8 grid of squares of alternating colors. Those properties directly affect the way the game executes, which would be fundamentally different if played on a 7×7 grid or a 9×9 grid. So it's important that all chessboards are structured the same way. Backgammon, sudoku, billiards, and professional basketball all similarly depend on the play space having a specific physical structure. Video games also have environmental boundaries; even though the walls of a fortress in *World of Warcraft* aren't physically real, the characters are nonetheless unable to pass through them.

In other games the environment can vary considerably, and may not even be designed, but still contains features that structure the way the game executes. No two golf courses are the same, but they all have tees, fairways, greens, holes, sand traps, and water hazards, all of which give shape to the gameplay. Hide-and-seek can be played nearly anywhere, but the number of places where people can hide themselves imposes constraints on players' choices.

Environmental constraints also include the artifacts that enable play, such as dice, playing cards, pawns, balls, and bats. These are often designed with exact characteristics that can't be changed. For example, a deck of cards has only four aces, no matter how much you might need a fifth one. Just choosing the number of six-sided dice that a game uses is a significant design decision (Figure 2.1). These physical characteristics play a significant role in giving form to games like craps and Monopoly, which rely on a combination of strategy and probability.

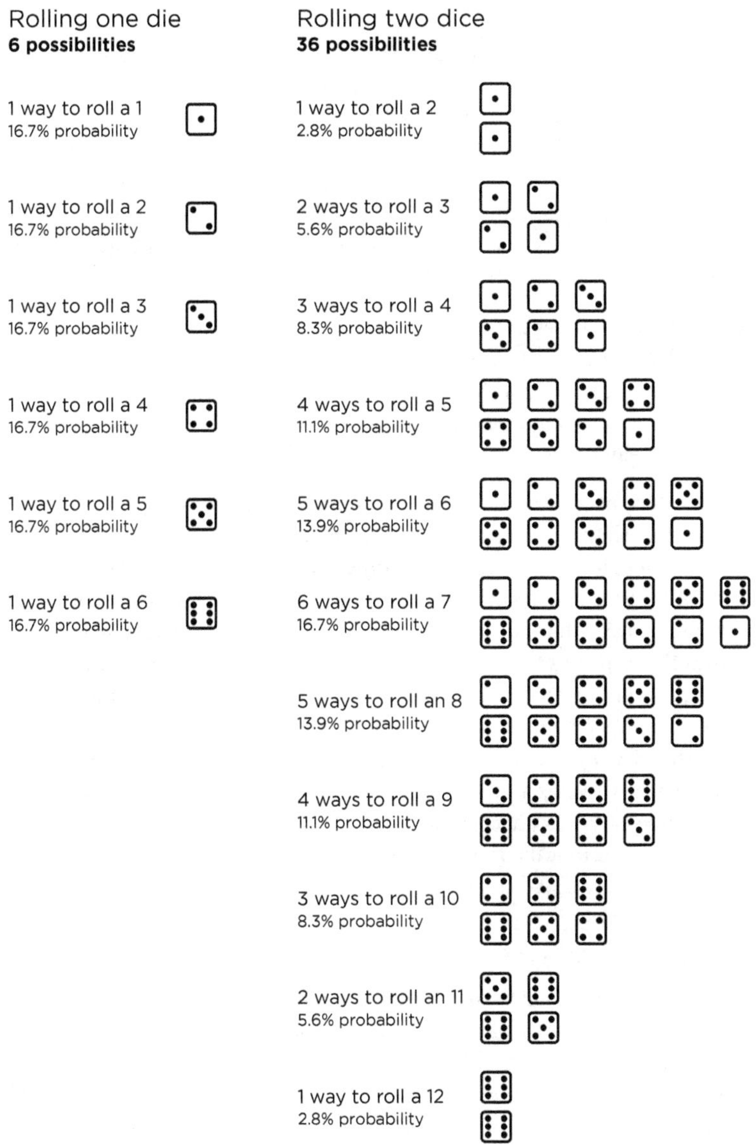

Rolling one die
6 possibilities

1 way to roll a 1
16.7% probability

1 way to roll a 2
16.7% probability

1 way to roll a 3
16.7% probability

1 way to roll a 4
16.7% probability

1 way to roll a 5
16.7% probability

1 way to roll a 6
16.7% probability

Rolling two dice
36 possibilities

1 way to roll a 2
2.8% probability

2 ways to roll a 3
5.6% probability

3 ways to roll a 4
8.3% probability

4 ways to roll a 5
11.1% probability

5 ways to roll a 6
13.9% probability

6 ways to roll a 7
16.7% probability

5 ways to roll an 8
13.9% probability

4 ways to roll a 9
11.1% probability

3 ways to roll a 10
8.3% probability

2 ways to roll an 11
5.6% probability

1 way to roll a 12
2.8% probability

FIGURE 2.1

One die creates 6 possible outcomes, each of which has an equal chance of occurring. Two dice create 11 possible outcomes, some of which are more likely to occur than others.

Games also formally constrain people's actions through their rules. Although such soft constraints serve a function similar to that of environmental constraints, they are fundamentally different because nothing keeps players from breaking the rules other than their mutual agreement not to do so. In the absence of hard physical constraints, people must volunteer to place limits on their own freedom. The players who join a game must, then, see some value in the experience. They're willing to submit to the game's formal constraints because they enjoy playing.

Although chess pieces themselves are an environmental constraint (you have only 8 pawns, not 9 or 10), chess as we know it wouldn't exist without the rules that govern how those pieces move. It's the interplay of the rules, the pieces, and the physical constraints of the board that make chess the distinctive game it is.

Because formal constraints rely on everyone choosing to honor the rules, there's the risk that people may cheat by simply choosing not to. Cheaters exploit other players' self-imposed willingness to abide by a set of rules, abusing their trust and robbing them of their right to the game's rewards. You might notice that the potential for this same kind of abuse is present in many other aspects of everyday life—business, relationships, education, and so on. More on this to come, but the point is that, in many games, the risk of cheating creates a burden on the players to police one another. However, game theorists Katie Salen and Eric Zimmerman point out that the fact that people cheat attests to the intrinsic value of a game experience. Cheaters aren't spoilsports; they accept that it's worthwhile to be seen as the winner of the game, but they flout the rules because they don't want to live by the same constraints that everyone else does.[1]

A Very Simple Example

In trying to understand the defining characteristics of games, it's helpful to start by looking at the simplest examples and then consider how they apply to games of all kinds. It's hard to get any simpler than rock-paper-scissors, and most people would agree that it is in fact a game. If a universal set of characteristics exists that binds all games together, then all those characteristics must be visible in rock-paper-scissors.

Objective

- The game's single objective is to select a value that trumps the value your opponent selects.

---

1 Salen, K., & Zimmerman, E. (2004). *Rules of play: Game design fundamentals.* Cambridge, MA: MIT Press, p. 275.

Environmental Constraints

- Players must select from one of three available values.

- Each player's hand is closed in a fist until his or her selection is revealed, preventing the other player from reacting to that selection.

Formal Constraints

- Players must reveal their selections simultaneously.

- Rock trumps scissors.

- Scissors trumps paper.

- Paper trumps rock.

These are all of the design elements needed to completely describe rock-paper-scissors, and they distinguish rock-paper-scissors from other games. The three types of characteristics listed here are present in any game, and they describe the essential mechanic at its root. Any other design choices are just matters of style.

Characteristics of Video Games in Particular

Video games, like all other games, contain each of the three characteristics just described. But they also represent a recognizable subclass of games that are both distinct from other types of games and coherent with one another. To define video games, we need to expand the elements specified in the model that I already laid out—objectives, environmental constraints, and formal constraints—to include one more characteristic that is specific to them.

Machine-Based Arbitration

All video games remove from human beings the burden of policing compliance with the rules and sorting out winners from losers. These things are all arbitrated by a machine. Other types of games have similar mechanisms for arbitrating play, including slot machines, pinball, and pachinko. Video games fall into that broader class of games, arbitrated through a computer instead of a physical mechanism (Figure 2.2).

This quality creates a huge design advantage for video games, because it allows the game's rules to be much more complex and to be executed much faster than would otherwise be possible. Calculating all of the variables that affect the outcome of a single battle in *World of Warcraft*, with multiple characters comprising many different attributes, issuing many different attacks, and equipped with many different types of armor, would be so laborious that the game would progress very slowly.

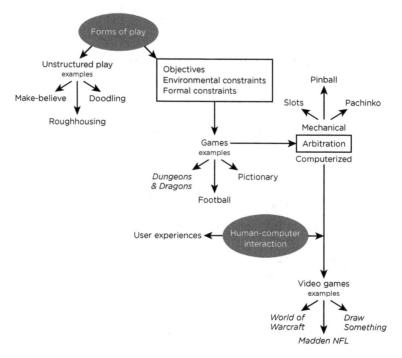

FIGURE 2.2
Video games belong to a subclass of games that have a means of arbitrating play.

With a computer handling all of that bookkeeping, players can speed through battles in real time. They can focus on the flow of events rather than the drudgery of calculation. So video games have a special capacity for modeling complex systems and making them playable, allowing people to experience things that would otherwise be impossible or too risky in very realistic ways. It's worth keeping this capability in mind when considering how video games can have relevance beyond pure entertainment.

Games in the Real World

The Magic Circle

Anthropologist Johan Huizinga described games as creating their own reality, walled off from the real world within what he called the "magic circle." When stepping into the circle, players agree to abide by the special rules of that world for the sake of the game experience, leaving the rules of everyday life behind (Figure 2.3).

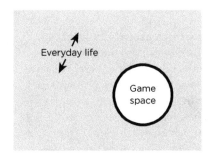

FIGURE 2.3
Huizinga suggested
that games are distinct
experiences from
everyday life, walled
off and secluded from
it in what he called the
"magic circle."

Huizinga emphasized that the circle is a hard boundary separating the game world from broader reality; nothing comes out of the circle into real life. He wrote, "Summing up the formal characteristics of play we might call it a free activity standing quite consciously outside 'ordinary' life as being 'not serious,' but at the same time absorbing the player intensely and utterly."[2] Huizinga's ideas have influenced contemporary theories of play and game design, and his writings reflect the broad cultural predisposition to classify games purely as diversions from real life.

I take the position that Huizinga was too absolute in disconnecting game worlds from our own. Games do indeed spin their own realities, but for our purposes it's better to think of the walls of the magic circle as permeable (Figure 2.4). Elements of the real world can enter the game space, where they can be processed and then returned as output back into real life. Thinking about games in this way opens the door to creating games that have real impact in the real world.

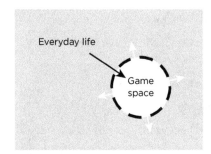

FIGURE 2.4
Games do create a
distinct reality, but
that doesn't mean they
need to be completely
separated from
everyday life.

2 Huizinga, J. (1950). *Homo ludens: A study of the play-element in culture.* Boston, MA: Beacon Press, p. 13.

Living Games

Earlier I made the case that a common set of characteristics defines all games. Taking that premise a step further, we can also think of anything that has all of those characteristics as a game, even if it's a part of what we would normally call real life. I'll give two examples: Ebay and classroom tests. Note that I'm not just saying that these things are game-like, or that they contain some elements of games, but rather that they are *indistinguishable* from games. We're just not used to thinking of them that way. Adopting this view is useful because the design of such things can benefit from the very same practices that make games so compelling. These are the best circumstances in which to apply game design, because they give you the opportunity to draw out the innate game-ness that already exists within an experience rather than attempting to tack it on.

Ebay Is a Game

Ebay is a great example of a system that we normally think of as a conventional user experience but that can be understood as a game. It shares all of the characteristics of video games that I've outlined.

Objective

There are two possible objectives in Ebay, depending on which role a person is playing.

- The buyer's objective is to "win" an item by offering the highest bid.

- The seller's objective is to get the highest price for the item.

Environmental Constraints

Ebay's system imposes hard limits on what players can and cannot do.

- Sellers can use only the capabilities available through Ebay's seller pages to entice buyers to submit bids for their items.

- Sellers can set a minimum reserve price for their items.

- Each auction expires at a set time.

- Field constraints force buyers to submit valid numeric bids.

- Similar items are available at the same time, along with information about when their auctions expire and what the current top bid for each one is.

Formal Constraints

Ebay has an extensive set of official rules governing people's behavior that are not constrained by any hard attributes of the environment. Among them are these:

- Sellers must truthfully represent the products they put up for bid.

- Buyers must honor their winning bids by paying sellers.

- Sellers must ship purchased items to buyers within a reasonable time frame.

Machine-Based Arbitration

- Ebay's system arbitrates auctions automatically, managing bids and assigning one person as each auction's winner.

- To the extent that it can, Ebay polices each auction for cheaters, monitoring whether payments have actually been made through PayPal. One way that people cheat on Ebay is by convincing sellers to settle their auctions outside of the system, and then failing to pay.

Ebay also benefits from some game-based reward systems. Players earn points for favorable ratings as buyers or sellers, and periodically level up to become more trusted participants. Ebay could push this system much further, adopting the same design practices and patterns that so powerfully drive people to develop their characters in games.

Tests Are Games

One field that's already leading the way in the application of game design is education, perhaps because it fits the definition of games so very well. Consider testing, for example.

Objective

- Earn the best possible grade on the test (a high score).

Environmental Constraints

- The questions that are on the test.

- The form of each question. Multiple-choice, matching, fill-in-the-blank, and true-or-false questions each impose a different type of constraint on the student.

- The amount of time allotted to complete the test.

Formal Constraints

- Students are not allowed to ask other students for answers or to look at other students' answers.

- Students are not allowed to leave the classroom during the test.

- Students are not allowed to use notes, books, calculators, or smartphones to look up answers (unless the teacher says otherwise).

If a test is administered by computer, it can even be described as a video game. Considering that people are naturally drawn to game experiences, it's a shame that testing is a source of anxiety for many students. The design of conventional tests fails to take advantage of their innate game-ness. The *Professor Layton* series for the Nintendo DS presents puzzles that are often similar to SAT questions, yet manages to be a wildly successful franchise (Figure 2.5). By conceiving of the experience first and foremost as a game, a reformed approach to the design of testing has the potential to transform education. I'll explore some of the ways that innovative thinkers are achieving this transformation in Chapter 12.

FIGURE 2.5
Professor Layton and the Unwound Future presents players with problems that require skill in geometry, mathematics, and logic.

Finding Useful Models

In this chapter I've presented a model for understanding games that can help UX designers perceive the game-ness of everyday experience. It's important to emphasize once again that there is no single, authoritative definition of games, and that there are considerable differences among different theorists. But arriving at a single truth is beside the point. The real value of any model is its usefulness. Understanding video games as systems of objectives, environmental constraints, formal constraints, and arbitration opens the door to creating real-world applications for games. As such, it is a useful model for this book.

CHAPTER 3

The Elements of Player Experience

In the last chapter I presented a model for understanding what it means for something to be a game. But designing enjoyable and meaningful games requires something more, something that provides a way of thinking about people's *experience* of games. Player experience is fundamentally different from the user's experience of the nongame user interfaces that we normally design. However, since UX and video game design are both centrally concerned with the quality of a person's experience as enabled by technology, UX designers have aptitudes that can lend themselves to the design of high-quality games. So we need a way of thinking about games that will allow us to transfer those existing aptitudes successfully.

One of the most familiar and useful frameworks in UX design is practitioner Jesse James Garrett's "elements of user experience,"[1] but that model is specific to the Web. We need a different model to understand and design for games. In this chapter I propose a similar framework for player experiences to help UX designers build games that are successful, engaging, and enjoyable. The model is divided into five planes, each of which is further divided into short- and long-term effects (Figure 3.1). Although simplified, this model provides a basis for thinking through the broad elements of design that work together to construct the effect of a game. Better development of each of these planes will result in a better game experience, and the quality of the experience would suffer if any of them were neglected.

FIGURE 3.1
Player experience can be thought of as comprising five planes. In better games, each of these planes is well developed.

Long-term
Contemplative
Sensory
Short-term
Aesthetics
Mastery
Control
Usability
Campaigns
Interactions
Balance
Strategy
Tactics
Meaningful choices
Rewards
Interest
Motivation

---

1   Garrett, J. J. (2002). *The elements of user experience: User-centered design for the Web.* Indianapolis, IN: New Riders, p. 21.

Motivation

In designing a game, it is critical to have a well-developed sense of who will be playing your game and why they would want to play it. The motivation plane comprises two main elements. In the short term, there's the up-front "interestingness" of the experience, the basic spark that grabs people and creates joy in the interaction. In *Pac-Man*, this is the race to clear the board while being pursued by enemies. In *CityVille*, it's the combination of creative control over the city and the challenge of managing its growth. In checkers and chess, it's the puzzle of figuring out how to attack your opponent while defending your own positions (Figure 3.2). These are all tied to basic human drives to complete a job, to create, and to feel competent, which are just a handful of the many motivations that make play a fundamental function of living. I'll discuss player motivations more extensively in Chapter 4.

MICROSOFT

FIGURE 3.2
The challenge of figuring out how to outwit your opponent makes chess fundamentally interesting.

The second element of motivation is the feedback of intrinsic rewards that sustains interest in the experience over time. *Pac-Man* has simple points and leaderboards. *CityVille* offers access to an expanding set of game items, coupled with a powerful social experience shared by a circle of friends. In checkers and chess, it's the satisfaction of proving that you're cleverer than your opponent. Rewards become increasingly important the longer a game runs, but they can also grow stale as the player gets used to receiving them. For very long engagements, diversifying and layering reward systems can persuade players to stay involved. See Chapter 10 for ideas you can use to construct such engrossing systems.

Meaningful Choices

The second plane defines how the game's structure and rules allow players to exercise choices that influence the outcomes of events. Such meaningful choices are present in all good games, though they can take very different forms. Chess relies heavily on long-term strategy, requiring successful players to anticipate possible future moves at each turn. Twitchy action games typically involve more short-range tactical decisions, which are completed rapidly and in high volumes at the fine motor level.

The challenge of consistently making the best moves is the fundamental conflict that makes play engaging. Games work best when there's a partial ambiguity between which actions will result in better or worse outcomes. *Pac-Man* takes place in a maze, where it's not entirely clear whether you'll get a better outcome by going left, right, up, or down at any moment. You can, however, maximize your chances of success by considering where the ghosts are, where the pellets are, whether a fruit bonus is available, and how many pathways for escape lie ahead (Figure 3.3). In this way, *Pac-Man* provides players with a good basis for making meaningful choices when the effects of any action are partially ambiguous. Games can easily lose their appeal when players either have no basis for distinguishing between choices (too much ambiguity) or only one choice that has any real merit (no ambiguity at all).

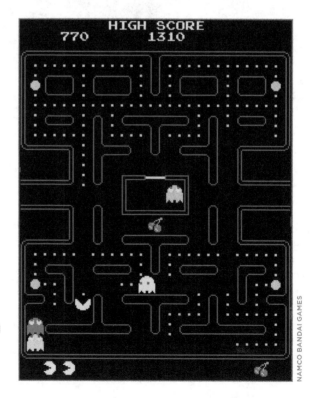

FIGURE 3.3
What move at this point would result in the best outcome for the player? Meaningful choices like these make *Pac-Man* an engaging game.

NAMCO BANDAI GAMES

Balance

Balance is the extent to which the game's elements work in combination to create a system that is appropriately challenging while still being perceived as fair and equitable. In an unbalanced role-playing game, for example, players might earn so much gold from easy battles that they could purchase the most advanced weapons and armor right away for use against the weakest enemies. On the other hand, if they earned too little gold, the game would demand too much repetitive work for too little reward and become frustrating.

Video games contain multiple variables that require a Goldilocks range of values—not too high or too low, but just right. But games are dynamic systems, and the interplay of these variables can be very complex and hard to completely anticipate. Even if a game works really well in a few scenarios, there may be lots of edge cases where it goes completely haywire and the experience becomes unsatisfying. The best way to ensure a balanced game is through iterative prototyping and testing, allowing the problems to emerge from actual play.

Games can encompass both short-term and long-term aspects of balance. In the short term there are basic interactions of the game, such as battles, in which the effects of balance can be seen relatively quickly. Paper prototypes, discussed in Chapter 7, can often reveal short-term balancing problems. In the long term, players may engage in campaigns that unfold over the course of the entire game. In role-playing games, for example, players are continually making decisions about how their characters will develop in terms of relative strength, intelligence, dexterity, and so on. Players should be able to pursue winning strategies at the game's end regardless of the path they've taken (though they may have made the task more difficult). If it became impossible to complete the game through some paths, the outcome of that campaign would feel intrinsically unfair. Identifying such potential long-term problems of balancing requires careful playtesting, which is the subject of Chapter 8.

Usability

Although the usability plane certainly includes all of the interface concerns that we know so well in the UX world, there are also some usability considerations that are specific to game experiences. The design needs to support a sensible experience so that players understand the things that happen in the game and can tell how their actions affect these outcomes.

This means that when players lose, they should understand why they lost; and when they win, they should understand why they won. When something happens in the game, players should be able to attribute it to a cause that they can perceive and understand. Players also should always understand the actions available to them, as well as the objectives they should be working toward (or they should at least have a reasonable opportunity to figure them out). These are the qualities that enable a feeling of control over the experience in the short term, and that allow players to master the game over time.

Aesthetics

The last plane encompasses the many aspects of the game's aesthetic design. In the short term, there's the direct sensory experience, which includes images, sound, and even the haptic elements of force feedback and vibrating game controllers. Stylistic choices in writing and art set the game's tone—whether it's funny, serious, foreboding, or silly. Many games also contain more contemplative elements that unfold over the long term, such as narratives with evolving story arcs.

A game's aesthetics can be readily changed without affecting the underlying mechanics governing play. You can swap out the standard black-and-white chess pieces with Civil War, ancient Chinese, or *Star Trek* figures, but you're still playing chess. So it's important that the underlying planes of the experience are sound, no matter how glossy the surface. Nonetheless, the aesthetic you use has a profound impact on the player's experience of the game. You can't peel the artful qualities of *Red Dead Redemption* or *Plants vs. Zombies* away from their game mechanics without completely changing each one's effect (Figure 3.4).

FIGURE 3.4
The quirky art style of *Plants vs. Zombies* is an important part of its player experience.

What about Fun?

You might be wondering where fun factors into this model. Fun is, of course, the most important quality of games, and the most compelling reason why people want to play. However, games can't be directly designed to be "fun" any more than a software experience can be directly designed to be "satisfying." If designers had access to a "fun" dial, it would be a simple task to crank it all the way up and make every game the most awesome game ever.

Unfortunately, it's not that easy. Instead, fun emerges from the experience when all of the elements work well together. Conversely, fun dies when any plane hasn't been adequately addressed. Fun is the consequence of sound game design. Understanding game experiences as planes of motivation, meaningful choices, balance, usability, and aesthetics allows us to focus on the qualities that create the feeling of fun.

CHAPTER 4

Player Motivations

W hy do people play games? It feels a little ridiculous to even ask this question, because the answer seems obvious: people play games to have fun. Do we really need a grand explanation beyond that? Well, if your interest in games doesn't extend beyond playing them, I'll grant you that the simple answer is probably enough. But for a game designer, there are at least two problems with such a basic explanation of player motivation.

For one thing, it doesn't account for the nearly masochistic things people are willing to do when playing a game. Many of the most popular role-playing games, for example, require players to fight the same enemies over and over again (and then again and again) to get the experience and loot they need to advance in the game (Figure 4.1). Players may spend dozens of hours in thousands of battles. So many games involve these kinds of endless repetitive actions that the gaming community has given it a name: *grinding*. This term is related to how we describe work we really don't enjoy—as "a grind." So why do people pay good money to subject themselves to something that's as unpleasant as the work an employer would pay them to do? This is a really big problem if your only explanation for why people play games is to have fun.

FIGURE 4.1
Role-playing games like *Final Fantasy XIII* involve countless battles against similar enemies.

Second, there isn't a clear definition of what we mean when we say "fun." Different people experience fun differently. A lot of people love riding roller coasters, but when I get on one I hope only for a swift death. Some people have a blast at work, while others would be tortured by the same job. There are even some people who don't have any fun at all playing video games. Because the concept of fun is so slippery, it can't help inform design decisions. You can't build a game to satisfy a need you can't define.

So, then, why are people so drawn to video games? What do they expect the experience of playing a game to provide? Human psychology provides a lot of insight into these questions.

Why Psychology Matters in Game Design

Jamie Madigan

One of the things I've discovered in applying the science of psychology to understanding video games is that it's a surprisingly short leap in logic. People who make games are dealing with human psychology, and an understanding of the theories and methods in that field are critical for crafting great experiences. Understanding psychology allows you to craft experiences better because it helps you predict what players will think and what they'll do.

Even little tweaks, like framing an outcome as a loss instead of a gain, or creating the illusion of progress toward a distant goal, can have huge impacts on how gamers behave, what choices they make, and how they feel about the experience. For example, when Blizzard wanted to encourage its *World of Warcraft* players to take more frequent breaks during long sessions (presumably to combat fatigue from gaming marathons), they made a change from a system that degraded experience points per kill the longer you played, to a system that amplified experience points during play that followed a long break. Players liked it a lot better, even though the math shows that Blizzard didn't actually change anything except to present the system as a gain instead of a loss.

Sure, a lot of designers reach these insights through trial and error or by paying close attention to what works, but even a cursory understanding of a few established theories can yield tremendous benefits. Every little decision a game designer makes will be encountered by a squishy human brain, and psychology is the science that allows you to understand what that brain will make of it without trying to re-create everything from scratch every step of the way. Countless professors, researchers, and hapless college sophomores trying to earn extra credit for their Introduction to Psychology classes have already blazed a path for you to stroll down.

Dr. Jamie Madigan is a psychologist who has written for Gamasutra.com, GamePro *magazine, and* The Industrial Psychologist. *He blogs at PsychologyOfGames.com.*

Common Motivations

Getting a handle on players' motivations is extremely important because it tells you what your game needs to accomplish to fulfill their expectations, and that in turn helps to inform design. It's very easy to fall into the trap of thinking that people will play a game just because it's a game and, well, people like games. If you approach game design with that mind-set, you run the risk of putting in a lot of effort to build something that no one will want to play. Any game experience is much more likely to be successful when its design is rooted in an understanding of why people would want to play it.

Unfortunately, there is no single universal reason why people play games, and a variety of (often competing) models have been proposed to describe player motivation. Part of the appeal of video games is that they can satisfy many different kinds of human needs and desires, which often overlap with few clear divisions to distinguish them. What follows is a partial list of common motivations that explain the appeal of many games. In each case I suggest some ways that games can be designed to satisfy that motivation. When creating a design, it's worth setting aside some time to think about which motivations your game will fulfill.

Immersion

Every dedicated gamer knows the experience of being deeply immersed in a video game. You're doing pretty well and really enjoying yourself, when you discover that hours have passed in what felt like minutes. Then you notice a terrible burning sensation in your eyes. You realize you've unconsciously stopped blinking, setting aside a real physical need to minimize the risk that something terrible might happen to your game self while you weren't looking. This kind of experience demonstrates the powerful capacity of video games to immerse people in an alternate universe where the concerns of everyday life disappear.

Under ideal circumstances, a deep experience of immersion in a game can lead to what psychology theorist Mihaly Csikszentmihalyi calls "flow," a state of heightened focus and engagement in an activity.[1] Flow may occur when you're running a marathon, mowing the lawn, or playing the piano. It's characterized by feelings of contentment and well-being, even euphoria. Players need to be reasonably skilled with a game before flow can set in. It won't happen when a player is new to a game, because new players are spending too much time just figuring out how to operate it. Once players are able to concentrate on the challenges of gameplay instead of the interface, they're primed for a state of flow.[2]

---

1 Csikszentmihalyi, M. (1998). *Flow: The psychology of everyday experience.* London, England: Harper Perennial, pp. 39–42.

2 Chen, J. (2007). Flow in games (and everything else). *Communications of the ACM, 50*(4), 31–34.

Psychologist Jamie Madigan proposes that designers can deepen the experience of immersion in a game by maximizing the *richness* and *consistency* of the game environment.[3] "Richness" refers to robust detail and depth in the game world, as well as the presence of challenges that are cognitively demanding. These qualities pull a person further into the experience. "Consistency" means that nothing breaks the illusion. Everything should abide by the rules of the game world, and behave as you would expect it to if you really lived in that world. Glitches in the programming, incongruous dialog, or gratuitous in-game advertising risks pulling players out of the game experience.

Many modern video games, like *Grand Theft Auto*, go to elaborate lengths to construct worlds of staggering richness and consistency (Figure 4.2).

ROCKSTAR GAMES

FIGURE 4.2
The urban setting in *Grand Theft Auto IV* is built to a remarkable level of detail, inviting the impression of a real living city.

You don't necessarily have to spend zillions to achieve a similar effect. Designers always depend on the player to enable the experience of immersion, because no game world is exactly like life as we know it. Players who desire to be immersed in an alternate reality are willing to suspend their disbelief and fill in the gaps.

Ultima, a series of open-world role-playing games from the 1980s, was very committed to creating a rich and consistent alternate reality, despite its very rudimentary graphics (Figure 4.3). Each edition in the series was

---

3   Madigan, J. (2010, July 27). The psychology of immersion in video games [Web log post]. Retrieved from www.psychologyofgames.com/2010/07/27/the-psychology-of-immersion-in-video-games.

set in an enormous world full of cities, towns, and dungeons containing large numbers of characters the player could talk to, befriend, or fight. The games came with physical maps, books, and trinkets lifted from its elaborate mythology (Figure 4.4). Parts of the game were even written in a fictitious alphabet the player needed to learn. Despite the limitations of the technology, *Ultima* invited players to escape into a parallel universe and lent support to those who were willing to take the leap.

FIGURE 4.3
Ultima IV: Quest of the Avatar, released in 1985.

FIGURE 4.4
The physical artifacts that came packaged with the *Ultima* games gave tangibility to their virtual worlds.

Autonomy

Some players enjoy games that offer them the freedom to exercise control over their own actions as they see fit. Real life can be very structured, with a regular daily routine and little room for rule breaking. It can be refreshing to play a game in which few formal rules apply, and the degree of autonomy that such a game gives its players is very strongly related to how much people enjoy playing it.[4]

The *Grand Theft Auto* games, for example, give players tremendous autonomy, allowing them to do whatever they want, whenever they want, in a game world that has few boundaries. Players can choose from a broad variety of missions, quests, and minigames that are available at all times. They can also decide just to hop in a car, cruise around the city, and flip through radio stations as they watch the sunrise. If and when they feel like it, players can go shopping for clothing, invest in real estate, gamble at a casino, go on a date, pick up taxi fares, rescue people in an ambulance, go on a murderous rampage, or deliver pizzas. The game has very little to say about what players should do, while ensuring that they can do nearly anything. Which action to take is left to the players' own discretion.

Contrast this design with games that offer players little freedom, like *Dragon's Lair*. This arcade game from 1983 invited the impression that players would be controlling the actions of a cartoon character—that players would have a great deal of autonomy in the experience (Figure 4.5). Instead, the gameplay consisted of a predetermined set of joystick movements that the player needed to execute at precise times to keep the prerendered video running. The game actually offered no control over how the events unfolded at all—a disappointment, considering that control of the experience is one of the greatest strengths video games have over other entertainment media.

BLUTH GROUP

FIGURE 4.5
Dragon's Lair gave the false impression that players could control the actions of a cartoon character.

---

4   Ryan, R., Rigby, C. S., & Przybylski, A. (2006). The motivational pull of video games: A self-determination theory approach. *Motivation and Emotion, 30,* 347–363.

Games built to appeal to autonomy as a motivation will impose the fewest possible restrictions on the player's freedom. Players should be, in a sense, on their own to determine what they do in the game, and not pushed along by the designer's hand. They should have the latitude to pursue multiple different objectives, explore the game world at their own pace, and employ multiple strategies to solve problems. Players may be able to assume different personas for their characters, as villains or heroes, fighters or healers. It's helpful, too, if players can skip elements of the game that don't interest them, and focus on the portions that they find most compelling.

Competence

Most people have experienced the joy of a job well done. It can come in ways both large and small, from launching an exceptional user interface to perfectly executing parallel parking. There's an intrinsic pleasure in the feeling of being really good at something. The satisfaction we get from conquering these challenges only grows more acute with greater levels of difficulty.

Psychologist Carol Dweck argues that people are sometimes driven by the desire to feel that they're competent actors within an activity, which she calls a "mastery orientation."[5] People with a mastery orientation care about developing their skills and abilities, and take a genuine interest in activities for their own sake.

Games that offer players a feeling of competence may become very difficult indeed, although excessive difficulty can also diminish the appeal of a game to casual players and limit its potential audience. A common strategy for avoiding this problem is to allow players to select the level of difficulty that they want for a session of play. Another effective tactic is to award players special capabilities, items, or features when they complete optional difficult goals as a means of acknowledging their superior skill, cunning, or dedication.

Games that cater to the need for competence can also benefit by offering opportunities to learn and practice in a low-stakes environment inside the game, giving all players the chance to acquire the skills they need to operate competently in the game. This setup is common in fighting games like *Tekken* and *Virtua Fighter*, which coach the player through the elaborate key presses required to execute different martial-arts attacks and defenses.

Catharsis

The drive to hit, kick, blow up, demolish, destroy, and dominate underlies many modern blockbuster games. While it may not be our most attractive side, the consensus among psychologists is that we humans are by nature

---

5   Dweck, C. (1986). Motivational processes affecting learning. *American Psychologist, 41,* 1040–1048.

an aggressive lot.[6] The stresses of everyday life can heighten our aggressive impulses, and video games can offer cathartic relief from these pent-up tensions through scenarios that aren't available in the real world. The conflict in a game can serve as a surrogate for the common struggles of living.

There are entire genres that allow game players to explore different flavors of catharsis, such as fighting games, shooters, and vehicular combat (cars with guns on them—yeah!). It's worth cautioning that these games tend to have much larger male than female audiences, and that violent themes can be very alienating to many people.

But games that satisfy the desire for catharsis don't necessarily need to be centered on bloodlust. Games can instead provide catharsis in more abstract ways. For example, defeating someone in a chess match is exercising a form of aggression toward an opponent, which is all the more pronounced by the gradual and humiliating attrition of the losing player's pieces. Ruthlessness is a great quality in a chess player.

Games designed to provide cathartic experiences should have a clear sense of winning and losing. Winning players shouldn't be denied the opportunity to gloat just because it's uncouth. Many games also give players access to a broad variety of powers that expand with time, inviting the feeling that they're growing stronger through their experience with the game. *The Mark of Kri*, for example, builds tension throughout the game by giving players access to weapons that each have distinct strengths and drawbacks in their range, power, or agility. In the final act players earn a hefty battle-axe that has all three advantages and no drawbacks, granting players the cathartic pleasure of dispatching scores of enemies as though they were cutting through butter (Figure 4.6).

SONY COMPUTER ENTERTAINMENT

FIGURE 4.6
The brutal battle-axe in *The Mark of Kri* relieves much of the tension built up over the course of the game.

---

6 Gleitman, H., Gross, J., & Reisberg, D. (2011). *Psychology* (8th ed.). New York, NY: W. W. Norton, pp. 473–478.

Accomplishment

Many people dream of doing great things in life but find themselves constrained by circumstances. Only a small number of people will be recruited into the NFL, make a great film, or fly into space. To pursue a dream seriously, people often need to take great personal risks. Abraham Maslow posited that we pursue such goals only after our basic physical needs are met,[7] but this is not always true. Some people are willing to give up steady work to start their own business or move to an expensive city to seek stardom. The real peril in these situations is that the person taking such an enormous risk might not succeed. Failure, then, not only robs people of their dreams, but can also diminish their basic quality of life. Some people embrace such risks, but for many more they are an impassable barrier to trying. People can, however, still crave the experience of personal glory.

Games can offer people great accomplishment while putting them at no real personal risk. A key to the appeal of such games is that players know it's at least possible to succeed (though it may be extremely difficult). Everyone has the potential to achieve greatness. Furthermore, people have the prospect of succeeding without taking on the kinds of risks that could cost them their basic sense of security.

Games that indulge people's need for accomplishment offer grand fantasies and great peril: saving the world, medaling at the Olympics, or rescuing the president from the deadly cyborg ninjas. They also celebrate the moment of victory, showing the player standing atop an Olympic rostrum or being awarded the Medal of Honor. Some games allow players to record and save their winning runs so they can later replay them and relive their moment of glory.

Social Image

Earlier, I briefly mentioned Carol Dweck's theory of motivation driven by a mastery orientation. This is only half of what she had to say on the subject. The other part of the theory holds that some people have a "performance orientation": they do something because they want others to have a favorable impression of them. This might mean that you want people to see you as smart, capable, or cool. People with a performance orientation are concerned with preserving or improving their social image.

This is often an important reason why children play games, and why they select the same titles their friends are playing. *Pokémon* allows players to differentiate themselves from one another by the monsters they've captured. Players can then pit their monsters against one another in battles, offering a kind of social preeminence to skilled players. For many kids, these games can become entangled with their feelings of self-esteem.

---

7   Maslow, A. (1954). *Motivation and personality*. New York, NY: Harper.

Although most grown-ups don't take games quite so seriously, social image is nonetheless an important motivator for many people, and there are common patterns of design that cater to that drive. Massively multiplayer online games like *World of Warcraft* allow players to compare themselves to one another by level, and friends playing *FarmVille* can visit one another's estates to see how many items they've been able to acquire. Such devices allow players to show off their skill, dedication, or seniority.

For players to feel that the social currency is meaningful, other people must have a sufficiently active interest in the game. So the game itself needs to be popular, preferably among people the player knows. Catering to the motivation of social image may be easier with games designed specifically for groups of people who know each other, such as coworkers or families, than in games designed for a general audience.

Social Interaction

Most games are played with other people. Monopoly, baseball, and poker were all designed as games that require more than one person to play. But video games can provide artificial competition, allowing players to experience these pastimes without the involvement of other human beings.

For many people, though, the social experience of Monopoly, baseball, and poker has always been an enormous part of their appeal.[8] Indeed, socializing with other people is often the point, while the game itself is just a pretext that gives people an excuse to get together. Single-player video games can indulge a human fascination with gameplay itself, but for some people that misses the rationale for playing in the first place.

Game designers aren't blind to all this, and they've devised many ways to build social interaction into the video game experience. Since as far back as 1972, home game consoles have been built to accommodate multiple controllers, allowing players to play side by side in real time. This living-room experience remains an important way to play video games today, as demonstrated by games like *Rock Band*. Online multiplayer games like *World of Warcraft* have allowed people to forge friendships online, interacting in real time but disconnected space. Social networking games like *FarmVille* and *Mafia Wars* have created new ways for friends to interact and maintain their relationships, even though they're disconnected from one another in both space and time. The game world serves as the common place of convergence.

Games can better appeal to the human need for social interaction when players have a stronger sense of one another's presence. Avatars help people visualize one another. In-game chat allows them to speak to one another. Guilds and friend lists help them stay connected.

---

8   Salen, K., & Zimmerman, E. (2004). *The rules of play: Game design fundamentals.* Cambridge, MA: MIT Press, p. 462.

Note, however, that you should be cautious when facilitating free-form interaction between people in online games, because it can become an avenue for offensive behavior or exploitation. Especially in games designed specifically for children, consider protections such as allowing players to chat only by choosing from a list of predetermined phrases.

Creativity

Although many games have themes of destruction, many others appeal to the human desire to create. Some games provide players with no objective other than to showcase their creativity and imagination.

Simulation games like *SimCity* appeal to the innate delight in constructing things by letting players build their own living societies from the ground up. *The Sims* allows players to create their own people, build houses for them to occupy, and spin stories around their lives. Games like *LittleBigPlanet* and *ModNation Racers* give players tools to build their own games and then post them online for other people to play (Figure 4.7).

Games appealing to creative instincts benefit by giving players a broad palette from which to design. Players should have enough latitude to create things that are recognizably distinct from other people's work. This flexibility needs to be balanced against ease of use, because creative people want to create, not get bogged down in negotiating the user interface.

FIGURE 4.7
An intuitive user interface allows players to easily build their own racecourses and share them online in *ModNation Racers*.

These games also benefit by giving players ways to showcase their creative work. Many games allow players to post their games to an online gallery, where other people can visit their creations and even play through the game environments they've built. Other games provide a way for players to snap "photographs" from the game, so that they can build memories of the things they've created and carry keepsakes of the experience with them into the future.

[Insert Your Own Motivations Here]

Play is a highly individual experience. There are some universal reasons why people play video games, but there are many more idiosyncratic motivations than anyone can fully account for. I've played various games because I think they have artistic merit, because I have a nostalgic connection to a series, or because I'm writing a book about them. For every motivation, there's a design opportunity. To create a successful experience, a designer needs to begin by asking, "Why would someone want to play this game?"

Games Are More Than Just Having Fun

Designers who want to build games or game-like experiences need to have a more robust understanding of why people play games other than simply to have some fun. That rationale is too vague to help us make better decisions about how to design games that people will be more likely to enjoy. Understanding the specific motivations that drive people to drop everything, sit down, and spend valuable time playing a game makes it more likely that designers will create an experience that players will *describe* as fun and worthwhile.

CHAPTER 5

Ten Tips for Building a Better Game

"**O**kay," you say, "I'm ready."

You're a seasoned designer with a long history of creating compelling user experiences. You see the advantages that games can offer to UX design. You like (maybe even love) the idea of building an iPhone game to serve as a tour of a historic park, a social media game for Facebook to organize a political campaign, or a freestanding Flash game to teach basic physics on an educational website. You even have a rough concept of what that game might be like. You may be in a position to get funding for the project within your company or to pitch the idea to a receptive client. You want to start putting your ideas down on paper, get development under way, and speed toward launch.

That's an awesome place to be. Vision and ambition are written into the opening lines of all success stories. But there are some risks to jumping in too quickly. Game development is very time-consuming and resource-intensive. It can be difficult to make a significant change in direction if you discover midway through development that some of your initial ideas aren't translating into the great gameplay experience you had in mind.

So before getting started and running with it, you need a primer to point you in the right direction, to steer you clear of the most common mistakes, and to maximize your chances of success. This is the chapter for you. Though the challenges of building an enjoyable game shouldn't be oversimplified, the 10 general guidelines I present here will at least help you refine your ideas and break through some of the common barriers that could otherwise hold back your design.

1. Games Need to Be Games First

This point may sound too obvious, but it can be very easy to miss. And missing it is often the undoing of a well-intentioned design. You can design games to teach and persuade (as discussed later), but if such real-world objectives supersede meaningful gameplay, they will undermine your chances for success. First and foremost, a game needs to be enjoyed.

The Schwab MoneyWise *It's Your Life* game has a noble mission: to convince people to save more money for retirement and other long-term objectives. Much like the original Game of Life board game, *It's Your Life* presents players with a number of choices between spending or saving money over the course of a simulated lifetime (Figure 5.1). At the end, players get a letter grade to represent how well they did.

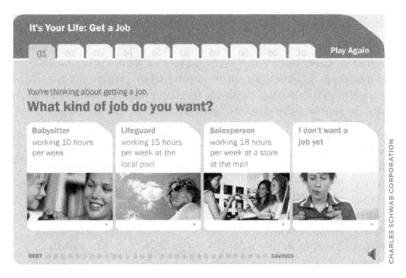

FIGURE 5.1

At each step in Schwab's *It's Your Life* game, it's pretty obvious which choice will lead to a winning outcome.

The problem is that the game's designers were much more interested in hammering home their message than creating an actual game experience. If you want to win the game, then the right choice each step of the way is to save your money and not spend any of it. Ever. On anything. That means you can earn an A+, the highest possible score, if you:

- Skip college

- Never move out of your parents' house

- Never get married

- Never have children

- Never travel or take any vacations

- Work indefinitely past age 65

- Die alone with lots of money and no one to leave it to

I'm sure the designers reasoned that people playing through the scenarios would elect to do valuable things with their lives, but they set up the game so that doing nothing with your life while saving vigorously is a sure way to win. Separating what people should do from what gets rewarded destroys the intended message. Even though *It's Your Life* is packaged as a game, it isn't committed to being experienced as a game.

2. Playtest, Playtest, Playtest

As much as we all know that testing is absolutely, completely indispensable in user interface design, I must stress (grammar be damned) that it is even more absolutely, completely indispensable when you're designing a game. Even though every UX designer's mantra is "test, test, test," it's still worth saying that you really must not neglect to playtest your game early and often.

The reason testing is so important in game development is that most video games are highly dynamic experiences. The flow of events changes from moment to moment, and each decision the player makes leads to a multiplicity of outcomes. Most games are also programmed with an element of randomness, so the same player never has quite the same experience twice. Multiplayer games throw even more unpredictability into the mix. As a result, the designer doesn't directly control the actual gameplay, but instead controls only the underlying system in which the play unfolds. Without actually seeing the game in action, you cannot reliably anticipate how it will work. Mike Ambinder, an experimental psychologist at game developer Valve Software, puts it in scientific terms: "Every game design is a hypothesis, and every instance of play is an experiment."[1]

So, aren't you fortunate to have a background in testing user experiences! Exploit it at every opportunity when designing your game. Grab your coworkers, your family, your friends—anyone who's willing—sit them down with your game, and watch them as they play it. Don't forget to play it yourself too! Be harshly critical. Do you enjoy playing it? When it's over, do you feel like playing it again? Is it frustrating? Is it boring? Is it too hard to figure out what to do? I'll go into more detail about game-specific testing methods in Chapter 8, but it's important that you be prepared to put your game under the microscope again and again, and to adapt the design to make it more enjoyable.

3. Games Don't Have to Be for Kids

Young people have much more leisure time than grown-ups, and many of us remember spending long periods of our childhood playing games. So it's natural for us to associate games with kids. Video games in particular tend to have a juvenile image, and that's not without reason: 91 percent of kids under age 17 identify themselves as gamers, and they often have a lot of influence over which games a household purchases.[2] Large segments

---

1   Phone interview with the author, January 21, 2010.

2   NPD Group. (2011, October 11). *The video game industry is adding 2-17 year-old gamers at a rate higher than that age group's population growth.* Retrieved from www.npd.com/wps/portal/npd/us/news/pressreleases/pr_111011.

of games are marketed toward children, and many of these games feature kid-friendly mascots like Pikachu or Mario. The link between childhood and video games is very real, so it's not surprising that designers often decide to create games specifically intended to appeal to children.

But with a large market catering to them, kids also have the latitude to be very discerning consumers. Enormously sophisticated cross-media marketing campaigns pushing big-budget titles already crowd one another out, so you'll find that just getting a young game consumer's attention is a tremendous challenge. Kids often select a popular title specifically because they feel it will raise their social status among their friends. Because these games can be very demanding of their time, your idea must offer a pretty compelling value proposition for them to sacrifice minutes or hours that could otherwise be spent with their pastime of choice. Kids take games seriously, and you can't assume that they'll play your game just because it's a game.

We also know that kids are only the minority of people who play video games. As I mentioned in Chapter 1, 82 percent of gamers are over age 18, and 29 percent are 50 or older (Figure 5.2).[3] Grown-ups can also be more receptive to playing games outside of the mainstream, and they have more disposable income to spend on games (if you plan to sell it to consumers).

This is not to say that kids couldn't make up a portion of your game's audience. But if your game is clearly intended for young children, as announced in breathless starbursts reading "Hey kids!" and "Super cool!" you will turn off the larger segment of gamers. So consider targeting your game to an older age group while keeping it accessible to a broad range of ages.

Video game players in the United States, by age

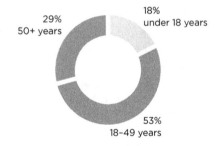

29%
50+ years

18%
under 18 years

53%
18–49 years

FIGURE 5.2
Kids under 18 represent the smallest minority of game players.

---

3   Entertainment Software Association. *Essential facts about the computer and video game industry: 2011 sales, demographic and usage data.* Retrieved from www.theesa.com/facts/pdfs/ESA_EF_2011.pdf.

4. Action Can Be Boring

Call of Duty: Modern Warfare 3 is an amazing action game. It unfolds over dozens of hours, during which you encounter waves of enemies exquisitely balanced against the resources available to you, interact with teammates controlled by artificial intelligence (AI) algorithms, and fight through varied locations that provide no unfair advantage to either you or your targets. And it's all wrapped up in an engaging and complex story line. *Call of Duty* also took years to make and a team comprising dozens of designers, artists, and engineers at a cost of many millions of dollars. You're probably not making *Call of Duty*.

It's very difficult to sustain adrenaline-pumping excitement for very long. If you do choose to make an action-based game on a small scale, you'll find that you're limited to very simple and short-lived scenarios that resemble games of the arcade era. Racing a car. Throwing a basketball. Shooting a spaceship. Taken on their own, these types of experiences tend to grow tiresome quickly. In comparison to the enormously sophisticated action games that people have access to today, they're just plain dull.

Consider what makes a game intrinsically interesting. You'll find a lot of creative opportunity in games that make the player think through interesting choices instead of executing twitch responses. The card game Hearts, for example, is all about choices (Figure 5.3). Which three cards should I pass to my opponent? Should I play a high card or a low card? Should I break hearts, or hold off to see if someone else does it first? If I play clubs one more time, will someone else stick me with the queen of spades? Should I try to shoot the moon, or will that prove self-destructive? Each choice is reevaluated from one trick to the next, depending on the changing conditions of your hand and on new information about what other players have already done. Even though Hearts can be a fairly long game, it can hold players' interest without any laser blasters or lava levels.

You can also invite players to apply their imaginations to the game. *Mafia Wars*, a Facebook game with more than 3.5 million monthly active players,[4] merely alludes to street crime while showing none of it (Figure 5.4). To pull off a bank heist, you just select "Bank Heist" from a menu of criminal activity. The game immediately responds with a message that you completed the job successfully. In place of real-time action and 3D graphics, players are offered choices about which jobs to take, how to invest their earnings, and which personal attributes to develop. There's no limit to what can be achieved in a player's imagination.

---

4 AppData.com, accessed November 19, 2011.

FIGURE 5.3
Hearts creates excitement by presenting players with lots of interesting choices.

FIGURE 5.4
Mafia Wars leaves the depraved criminality to the player's imagination.

5. Fit the Game into the Player's Lifestyle

Think about the real-life contexts in which people will play the game. Start the design process by asking:

- Who are your players?

- How much time do your players have to give to the game, and how much of that time would they actually be willing to give?

- Will your players need to take a break from the game and continue it later?

- How will your players access the game?

- Where will your players be when they're playing the game?

- What kind of hardware, software, and Internet access will be available to your players?

The answers to these questions can help you set requirements for the duration of play, the way the game will be accessed, and the technical requirements of players' computers and devices. Use playtesting to figure out whether your estimates are working out.

For example, Unisys developed a series of online games for the company's sales team to send to customers as holiday greetings. Customers would receive a link by e-mail to an online holiday card with a personal message from the salesperson. The card would then open out into the game, branded with the Unisys logo (Figure 5.5).

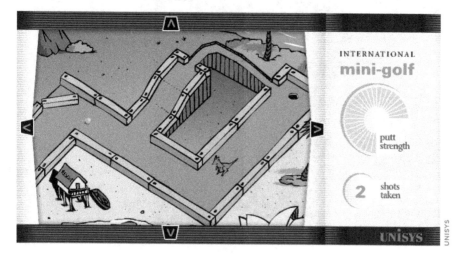

FIGURE 5.5

The Unisys mini-golf game was designed to be a quick, unintrusive diversion from the workday.

Because the players were adults receiving these e-mails at work, the games couldn't require a significant investment of time to reach the end, so all of them were designed to last less than five minutes. And because many players would be accessing the game while sitting in standard office cubicles, where they typically would have their computer speakers turned off to avoid irritating coworkers in their shared space, the limited sounds in the games were not essential to the experience.

Contrast that design with *Metal Gear Solid 4: Guns of the Patriots*, a home console game containing cutscenes (in-game movies during which gameplay is suspended) that can run as long as an hour and a half and can come at any time during play (Figure 5.6). Games like this ask for a real commitment from their players, and they are appropriate only for audiences with abundant leisure time.

FIGURE 5.6
Individual cutscenes in *Metal Gear Solid 4* could run an hour and a half.

FarmVille cleverly makes itself adaptable to the player's lifestyle. Players need to dedicate only a few minutes to it at a time, during which they can plant seeds for crops that take different amounts of real-world time to harvest. Raspberries take just two hours, so they're useful when the player can check in several times in a single day. Eight-hour pumpkins fit in well just before and after a workday. Crops like artichokes take four days to harvest—better for players who can check in only now and then. The player is asked for some commitment, as fully grown crops that are left unharvested for too long wither and cost the player gold coins. But the staggered growth rates allow the time commitment to be on the player's own terms (Figure 5.7).

FIGURE 5.7

The staggered harvest times for crops in *FarmVille* allows players to decide how much gameplay they can fit into their lives.

6. Create Meaningful Experience

Players have to apply their time, their concentration, and their problem-solving abilities to the challenges your game throws at them. There should be a point to these efforts, a payoff for their investment. When the game ends, players should come away feeling that the experience was meaningful.

For the game to be a meaningful experience, players need to have a sense of control over the outcome. If players win or lose, does that prove anything about their skill, knowledge, or cleverness? Or does it all just come down to a coin flip? Many games involve some element of randomness, putting parts of the experience beyond the player's control. A random element adds interest to the game by putting the outcome in doubt. But a meaningful game at least gives players a hand in tipping the odds in their own favor.

A great example is the card game Killer Bunnies, in which success is ultimately determined by a card picked randomly from a deck (Figure 5.8). The player who holds the match for that card (the "magic carrot") is declared the winner. No player has any control over which card is picked; it's a completely random selection. But the gameplay does give players some control over which matching cards they hold. Players compete for carrot cards over the course of the game, and shrewd players will work to hold the greatest number of them before the game is over. Even for the players who don't win, the game says a lot about their mastery of the strategy, tolerance for risk, and skill at reading other people. Players come away from the game knowing that they had control over their chances of success, which makes the experience meaningful.

FIGURE 5.8
Players exercise control over the outcome of Killer Bunnies by acquiring carrot cards, increasing the probability that they'll capture the randomly selected magic carrot.

7. Don't Cheat

Because video game rules are enforced inside the black box of the computer's circuitry, there's a particular temptation for designers to take shortcuts by letting the game cheat. Giving the system more information or control than the player has, for example, can be a simple way to build challenge into a game. Power in a video game is unbalanced between the computer and the player, and the player has no way of challenging the computer or holding it to account. Don't be tempted to cheat. It's a bad design choice because, first, people will be able to tell what's happening (oh yes, they will); second, cheating is a serious offense in games, and players have an instinctive revulsion to it.

Suppose you're designing a blackjack game that matches a player against a computerized dealer. As a designer, you need to write a script to control the dealer's actions. You want the dealer to be a little hard to beat but not impossible. One easy way to create challenge would be to let the script choose which card from the deck is drawn next. You then program the dealer to pick a card that will either win or lose, and put in a randomizing function so that two out of every three times it picks a winning card. This strategy also creates an easy way to allow players to change the difficulty, so that on a harder setting the dealer will pick a winning card four out of every five times, while on an easier setting it wins just one out of every three. Since the deck of cards displays facedown on-screen, how would anyone even know that you're cheating?

After playing the game a few times, you'll see how (Figure 5.9). The dealer will do seemingly irrational things, such as hitting on 20 and magically drawing an ace. The deck will not seem random, because certain cards will tend to show up early and others will show up only after those preferred cards have been drawn. After several playthroughs, these patterns will become painfully obvious. Although the player can't catch the computer in the act of cheating, these telltale artifacts are hard to cover up. When players realize that a game is cheating, they'll make the ultimate winning move by turning it off.

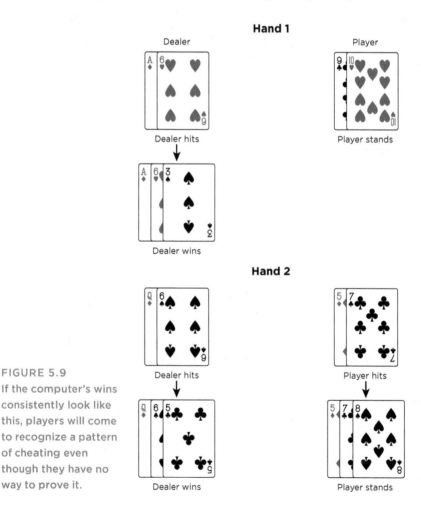

FIGURE 5.9
If the computer's wins consistently look like this, players will come to recognize a pattern of cheating even though they have no way to prove it.

A better approach is to build a simple, rules-based AI. Don't be too intimidated by the idea of building an AI; ultimately it's just a computer program like any other. In this case, all you need is a line of code that tells the dealer to hit on 16 and stand on 17. The important thing is that the computer is subject to the same rules as the player. Make things work the way they look like they should work. If you show a deck being shuffled, randomly pick the full sequence of cards and put it into an array that can't be changed. Don't let the AI know what card is coming up next, or what cards are in the player's hand. Don't abuse the inherent advantage you have as the game designer.

8. Skip the Manual

The best way to convince people a game is worth playing is to let them jump in and try it out for themselves. You can take people's decision to open a game as the clearest possible signal that they're in the mood to play, not to sit and read about how to play. Relying on written instructions presented at the beginning of every new game only creates a barrier to entry at the very time you want to be most accommodating of players. Instructions can also become a crutch, used to justify unconventional and unintuitive choices in the interface. Finally, game instructions can be very difficult to follow. Each game interface introduces a new vocabulary and a new set of controls. These things can be difficult to picture abstractly outside the dynamics of gameplay.

So the best place to teach people how to play a game is right there, inside the game itself. Tutorials have become one of the most familiar patterns in games. Minimalist, just-in-time instructions are even better (Figure 5.10). Ask yourself, "What's the smallest amount of information the player needs to make the first move?" Then provide nothing more than that; you can get to the second move when the time comes. Play is learning. If people are interested in the game, they'll be motivated to fill in the blanks themselves by playing it.

COURTESY OF BRI LANCE

FIGURE 5.10
In Bri Lance's game *Kanyu*, step-by-step instructions about how to play are cleverly incorporated directly into the game's story line.

And keep in mind that if your game needs robust instructions for people to play it, this may be a warning sign in and of itself. Your game may be too complex, and some simplification may be in order.

9. Make the Game Make Sense

Players need to understand why things happen in the game to feel that they're in control of it. Your skills as a UX designer will be very valuable here, because this point is fundamentally about the intuitiveness of the gameplay. In game design, building a sensible experience relies on some key understandings between the designer and the player.

- **When players lose, it should be clear why they lost.** If it's not, then players won't be able to get better at the game by avoiding the same mistake in the future. If this happens repeatedly, players will begin to feel that they're being unfairly punished.

- **When players win, it should be clear why they won.** If not, then it'll be hard to replicate the victory. A win that doesn't make sense can also cheapen the experience, leaving players feeling that the game's standards weren't that rigorous in the first place.

- **Every effect should have a clear cause.** When something happens, players should be able to understand why it happened. *Foldit*, discussed in Chapter 1, is a wonderful example of game mechanics applied to a real-world problem. The relationship between cause and effect, however, is often unclear in the game. Twisting a protein's side chain can create a conflict, but twisting a similar one in a similar way can earn you points. Trying to figure out why these actions have different results can be tremendously frustrating.

- **The object of the game should be clear.** Players need to know what they're working toward. A clear goal gives structure and meaning to the experience. It allows players to formulate strategies and gives them a reason to engage with the game. From the start and throughout every moment of play, players should be aware of their ultimate objective.

- **Players should always know what actions are available.** At every moment, visible or aural cues should be provided to let players know what they can do. Adventure games, a popular genre in the 1980s, were plagued by failures of basic intuitiveness, because they often forced players to guess at what arcane actions might be available. Using a blue key to open a blue door makes sense to most people; using your athletic supporter as a slingshot to knock out a guard (as was required in *Space Quest II*) really doesn't.

10. Make It Easy to Try Again

When you're down in the weeds constructing your game's mechanics, it's easy to focus on the ideal case in which players play straight through from beginning to end. It makes sense to author a game as a continuous narrative, with a beginning, a middle, and an end. But thinking of your game in those terms also risks losing sight of how it will actually be experienced in the real world. Remember to step back and think about the game as a discontinuous and iterative experience.

When a player loses, it should be easy to cycle back into the game and try again, instantly and effortlessly. Even large commercial games with multimillion-dollar development budgets make the common mistake of forcing a lengthy loading screen into that anxious space between a loss and a second attempt. Stretching that space of time to the second, third, or twentieth go-round inevitably tries the player's patience. Games like *Braid* and *Prince of Persia: The Sands of Time* have taken a clever route around this problem, allowing players to rewind time to a safe point before the losing moment.

Think, too, about the amount of work the game asks players to invest in it, and whether players would be frustrated if they lost and had to start all over again. This alone could be enough to make some players decide it's not worth returning to the game. Consider giving players the option to save their progress.

Think about giving players incentives to play the game again after they've completed it. Some common ways of doing this include:

- Simple performance yardsticks, such as the ratings on a carnival strength test

- Collectables and achievements earned throughout the game, and a tally of how many the player has managed to obtain

- Score tracking and online leaderboards

- Periodic releases of fresh content

- New features and privileges that become available only on successive playthrough

When people replay a game, they're signaling a personal appreciation for its design. Tracking the number of times people replay is one of the best general measures of your game's success.

Play to Your Strengths

These 10 guidelines will help you get started, but plenty of challenges lie ahead as you set about designing and developing your game, and you'll need to learn how to manage them as they come up. One last piece of advice is to play to your strengths. If you have a background in the design of conventional user interfaces, by all means use the skills and techniques that arise from it. Wireframing, user testing, rapid prototyping, storyboarding, flow diagramming, and other core skills all translate well to game design and can help you pull through the inevitable rough patches. When a game design issue has you confounded, trust your instincts and ask how you would handle a similar problem if you weren't designing a game. More often than not, you'll find that you can point yourself in the right direction.

CHAPTER 6

Developing a
Game Concept

I wish I could say that the hardest part of game design is just getting started. Unfortunately, design, development, testing, and promotion can also get pretty hairy. Still, developing the initial creative vision for a game is a significant hurdle to clear. Doing so successfully is the first step (of many) toward creating a great game experience. More to the point, great games cannot happen without a good vision.

This chapter encourages you to build your vision by thinking about your game from several different perspectives, and by posing questions that will help refine a budding concept into a more robust treatment with qualities conducive to good player experiences. At the end of the chapter I lay out a method for combining these perspectives in a generative fashion that will allow you to be discriminating in selecting the ideas that you believe hold the greatest potential for success.

Your Objective

The first question to ask is, Why do you want to create a video game? It's important to remember that any successful game's ultimate purpose must be to entertain its players; that's why people invest their time in the experience. It's possible that you have no objective beyond this, and that you view game design as a form of altruism or a means of artistic self-expression. There's great legitimacy in such ideals, but since this book is targeted toward UX designers, I assume that most readers are working in support of external objectives, most likely driven by business needs or by social causes. Understanding these objectives means getting a handle on your personal investment in the game.

It's also important to consider why you believe that a game is the best way to achieve your objective. Recognize that games are better suited to certain objectives, and entirely unsuited to others. Ask yourself where your objective falls on this spectrum, and what specific advantages games provide that cannot be met through other channels.

Common Objectives

Typically, objectives fall into one of a few common categories.

To Generate Revenue

For commercial video games, the designer's objective usually is to make money. The traditional gaming market is highly saturated and dominated by a few well-resourced companies, and I'm not assuming (or advising) that UX designers try to compete in that market. But there is a growing demand for niche gaming applications among businesses, schools, government agencies, and nonprofit organizations. In these cases, your objective to generate revenue would share space with the client's objective to achieve a different goal.

In any event, you'll need to think through the revenue model for your game. The model may include:

- Consulting fees paid by a client for the design and development of the game

- Direct sales of a packaged game to players

- Sales of licenses to the game to organizations that can benefit from its use

- Subscriptions that allow individual players access to the game for a specific amount of time or usage

- Ongoing sales of expansions to the original game

- Limited free play that requires payment for additional equipment, skills, or in-game currencies

- In-game advertisements

To Encourage Action

Games can be a highly effective way to elicit action in the real world, such as exercising more often and more vigorously, or adopting more fuel-efficient driving habits. In Chapter 11 I discuss how games can be designed to encourage these actions.

To Support Learning

A substantial and rapidly growing industry is dedicated to creating games that educate and train people. I cover such applications in depth in Chapter 12.

To Persuade

Games can be a wonderful way to convince players to adopt a particular point of view. See Chapter 13 for a complete discussion.

Your Players

The most important factor in the success of a game is how well it serves the people who play it. Creating a game that fits your potential players requires understanding who they are and why they value playing games. The usual methods that UX designers invoke to gain insight into their target users—including surveys, focus groups, interviews, ethnographic observation, and personas—are no less valuable in game design.

It's important to consider your players across several classifications. In each case, identify the full range of remotely plausible player groups, as well as the most likely player constituencies.

Classifying Player Groups

Demographics

How old are the players? Are more of them likely to be male or female? What's their level of education? How well do they understand the language in which you're writing the game? Do they have any motor, sensory, or cognitive impairments? Each of these questions will have different implications for the themes, challenges, length, and level of support provided in the game.

Motivation

Why would people want to play the game? It's not enough to say simply, "Because it's a game." People have a vast number of games to choose from. Why do you believe people will take an interest in your game in particular? Survey the people in your target audience about the types of games they like to play and why they enjoy them. Look for themes like those described in Chapter 4. Then consider which factors you can incorporate into your game's design to draw the interest of players and to sustain their interest over time. Will the game appeal to people who value social interaction, puzzles, playing with language, cutting-edge graphics, or compelling story lines? How do these priorities match up with the demographics you're targeting?

Skill and Comfort with Games

How much experience do your players have with video games? Are they people who spend dozens of hours every week in virtual worlds, or do they do a little casual gaming once or twice a week? Are you offering games to people who have had no real exposure to them before? Consider how the answers to these questions should influence the complexity of the gameplay and the controls. A design that's too simple won't suit hardcore gamers, but any significant complexity could completely exclude the least skilled players. Which group constitutes the larger portion of your likely audience? Are there ways to design the game so that it could appeal to a broader segment of players—such as allowing people to play at a level that's comfortable for them?

Access to Technology

How will people play your game? Do players have access to a personal computer? If so, what platform? How sophisticated is the hardware? Will they be playing the game in a location where they have access to the Internet? How likely are they to own a smartphone, a tablet, or a handheld gaming system, and how likely are they to carry it around? Do they have a home game console? Think about the effect that the available technology will have on the gameplay. For instance, games that require a full keyboard or a large screen can't go mobile, but games that require continual access to the Internet work especially well on mobile platforms.

How much time do players have on their hands? How many of your players are young people with time to kill, and how many of them are older people with families and jobs that demand most of their attention? Will the game be promoted through an organization, such as a school or business, that will carve out time for people to play? If there is no such organizational accommodation, consider how much of a commitment players would be willing to make or could be persuaded to make to your game.

The Conflict

Every game is built around some form of conflict. Conflict is created by the relationship between what players want to achieve (the objective) and the things that stand in their way (the environmental and formal constraints). This relationship sets up the central struggle of the game and constitutes a fundamental component of the game's design. Defining the conflict or conflicts that lie at the heart of the gameplay will guide many of the design decisions that follow.

Examples of Game Conflicts

- **Blackjack:** Draw a higher total card value than any of your opponents without going over 21. To win, players need to understand how to play the odds and fight the compulsion to take excessive risks.

- **Mastermind:** Deduce the color sequence created by your opponent in 12 guesses or fewer using the feedback that your opponent provides about each of your previous guesses. Players need to employ logic to win.

- *Frogger:* Consistently time your movements from one safe spot to another until all of your frogs reach the opposite side of the screen. Players need to have quick reflexes to win.

- *Qix:* Box out areas of the screen without allowing any part of the box you're drawing to come into contact with the randomly moving Qix. Players need to be able to think strategically and judge spaces and distances well to win.

- *Dance Dance Revolution:* Tap the right squares on a floor mat at the exact moment indicated on-screen, with greater accuracy than your opponents. Players need to have physical agility and a sense of rhythm to win.

Brainstorming Game Conflicts

How can you come up with the seed idea for the conflict of a game? Some key characteristics of the conflict examples listed in the previous section translate directly into guidelines for brainstorming.

- The design of the conflict has little connection to the game's presentation. Don't be too concerned with your game's look and feel, at least not right away. Many possible faces can be put on a game, and you can worry about that later.

- The conflict is the central activity of the gameplay, on which players spend most their time. Decide where you would like them to devote their energy. Do you want to force players to stop and carefully puzzle through their next move as in Mastermind, or pressure them to make the next move very quickly as in *Frogger*?

- The effect of each game is directly connected to its conflict. Imagine different effects that you would like the game to have on players. Should it pit the rational mind against the emotional mind as in blackjack, or should it promote a state of flow as in *Dance Dance Revolution*?

- Game conflicts can draw on a broad range of human abilities. Think about the different player abilities that your game could draw on. Should it stress spatial relationships as in *Qix*, logical reasoning as in Mastermind, or moment-to-moment reflexes as in *Frogger*?

Considerations in Developing a Conflict

Suppose you've brainstormed a list of possible conflicts. How do you distinguish between the good ones and the ones that are destined to go nowhere? There are several criteria to consider.

Interest

After people get past the graphics and the story line, they'll spend most of their time negotiating the game's conflict. So it's worth developing something that will make the time spent playing feel worthwhile. Much of the appeal of *Tetris*, for example, comes from the fact that its conflict is fundamentally interesting: fitting blocks together in the most efficient way without running out of space to manipulate them (Figure 6.1). This conflict appeals to people's natural interest in order, geometry, and the struggle against mounting adversity. If you have a game idea, ask yourself what makes its conflict interesting.

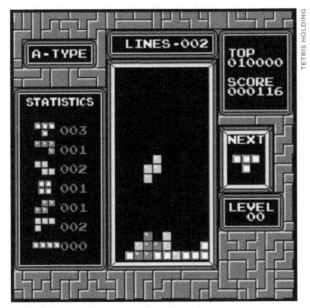

FIGURE 6.1
Despite its simplicity, *Tetris* has an intensely interesting conflict at its root.

Fairness

Think about whether the conflict gives the players a fair chance of prevailing. Remember that in video game design, the system always has inherent advantages over the players because it's the final arbiter of the rules. It's easy for people to become frustrated with a game that's overpowered and to perceive it as unfair. In multiplayer games, people need to feel that they have roughly equal chances relative to one another. People usually expect games to function like a meritocracy, awarding victory on the basis of an individual's skill, cleverness, or ruthlessness. For example, games that allow players to pay for certain advantages risk violating a core value of gaming, because most people believe it's unfair to pay to win. Ask yourself whether your game is fair to its players, and whether it fairly distributes power between opponents.

Complexity

The more complex a challenge is, the greater its demands will be on the player's attention. The conflict in chess, for example, is relatively complex. The objective to capture your opponent's king is complicated by the constantly shifting configuration of pieces. Bocce, by contrast, is relatively simple: try to throw the colored balls as close as possible to the white ball. A complex conflict can draw players deeper into a game, but it can also be exclusionary. Compared to chess, bocce is much easier for a novice to pick up and succeed at.

Sustainability

The conflict needs to keep people playing for the intended duration of the game. Consider the factors that could make the experience too short-lived. Is it possible for players to completely surmount the game's conflict too quickly, and be left with nothing to do? Does the conflict come to an end when the player finishes the game, or can players reconfigure the game and start over? Also think about whether the game could run too long. What are the chances that players will become stuck and be unable to continue? Repetitive conflicts in games, such as fighting the same enemies over and over, can grow tedious. Do you think that players could become bored and drop out of your game before completing it?

Duration and Lifetime

Using the information you have about the available time your players have to play, set objectives for how long the game should run. There are a few questions to consider when you're deciding on the game's duration and lifetime. Where you can, quantify your answers to the questions in each of the following sections in specific units of time (hours, minutes, or seconds).

Time to Complete

- What is the total duration of a *concise game*—that is, a game completed in the minimum number of turns by expert players?

- At the other extreme, how long could it take novice players to complete the game?

- Do you expect most people to fall somewhere in the middle? Are you shooting for a typical duration of play, or will it vary widely?

- Is there an element of the gameplay that places a limit on how long it can run?

Number and Duration of Sittings

- How long do you expect a single sitting with the game to last?

- How many sittings will it take to complete the game?

- Will the player be required to revisit the game frequently? For example, in *Words With Friends* (an online version of Scrabble), players forfeit the game if they wait more than one week to make a move.

- If the game is being developed for an organization to use internally, are there desired limits on how long a single sitting should be, and how frequently people should be able to play?

- If players take a long break from playing, how difficult will it be to re-join the game and get back into the swing of things?

Replay Value

- Will the game typically be a onetime experience, or will players be able to revisit it?

- How will the game entice people to play again after completing it?

End State

Win, Lose, or Tie

Perhaps the most familiar end state in a game is winning, losing, or tying against the system or other players. Ending the game in one of these states provides a feeling of completion to the experience. These states can be used in games that run for either short or long durations. They also provide a logical point at which players can decide whether to play again.

But these three states aren't the only ways that a game can progress. Particularly with video games, there are two other common scenarios.

Inevitable Loss

Some games don't have a winning condition and instead end when the player fails in some way. This was the norm in classic arcade games like *Pac-Man*, *Donkey Kong*, and *Tetris*. These games needed to come to a conclusion quickly enough to draw more quarters or to allow another player the chance to play. If your game needs to be similarly short-lived, then consider a mechanic in which players are bound to lose eventually.

Open-Ended Games

Some games never come to a formal end. In *The Sims*, for example, play doesn't stop until the player loses interest in it (Figure 6.2). You might design for this scenario if you want to create an enduring experience for players that they can come back to over and over again indefinitely.

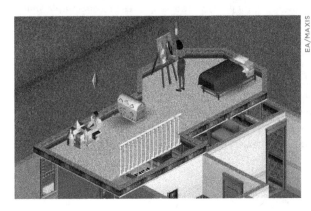

EA/MAXIS

FIGURE 6.2
Players can go on playing *The Sims* indefinitely, as long as they keep finding interesting things to do.

Player fatigue is a factor in open-ended games. As a designer, you'll need to develop ways to sustain interest in the game over time. For example, you could introduce new quests or expand the game environment, but such approaches can become burdensome. See Chapter 10 for a discussion of reward systems that can help keep people engaged in the experience.

Also consider how feasible it will be for your target audience to engage in your game on an ongoing basis, given their lifestyle. If sustained engagement is feasible, then focus on why players might feel motivated to return to the game. For players of *The Sims*, the motivation is the opportunity to create new homes and people to live in them. For players of *World of Warcraft*, it's the feeling of competence gained by completing quests and leveling up. In *CityVille*, it's the shared social experience with friends.

Linearity

Single Path

Many games prescribe a single path through the experience, presenting their challenges in a sequence that varies very little or not at all from one player to another. The advantage of the single path is that it gives you, the designer, greater control over how the gameplay unfolds. At every point you know what the player has already encountered and what is yet to come. And because there is a controlled set of use cases and test cases, development may also be simpler.

However, games that offer only a single path also reduce the players' freedom. If the feeling of autonomy is an important motivation for your players, they might find such a game overly limiting. Very linear games also sacrifice some replay value, because after a single pass the player has already seen everything there is to see.

Multiple Paths

Some games allow players to proceed through events in any order they wish. *The Sims*, for example, does not prescribe any sequence in which things must happen. As a result, the game is filled with a sense of personal freedom, and no limits are placed on its replay value.

Absolute nonlinearity can be difficult to achieve in any game that has a formal ending. The *Grand Theft Auto* games, for example, are in one sense very nonlinear because they allow players to go anywhere they like, anytime they like, in a massive virtual world. But these games also contain linear narratives that consist of a sequence of events culminating in a finale. Instead of pursuing nonlinearity to a fault, many games offer multiple paths to completion that are varied but nonetheless finite.

Player Interaction

Multiplayer games are wonderful for organizations like businesses and schools, where they can promote collaboration and where the designer can be assured of an installed base of players. If you're brainstorming a multiplayer game, there are several dimensions that will define the experience. Incidentally, many of these apply also to games played with virtual characters, or to the machine itself in a single-player game.

Number of Players

How many people will be interacting in the game at once? Different numbers of players have different social effects.

- Two-player games unfold like conversations between individuals, creating an intimate sense of a communal experience. Both players must be very engaged in the experience for the gameplay to succeed.

- Games played with small groups in which each player acts independently, such as poker, create both interactions between individuals and interactions with the whole group. There is enough room for players to have differing levels of engagement in the game, but not so much that individuals can go unnoticed.

- Breaking small groups into small teams promotes connectedness within the teams, as they learn how to work together against shared rivals. People can also play differentiated roles within a group, which can invite more inclusive participation. Children, for example, can play alongside adults without feeling that they're at a disadvantage.

- Games played with large groups, such as football, usually need team structures to keep the gameplay organized. Cooperation between individuals is then inherent in play. Some players can be less engaged without causing the game to fail, although team dynamics create pressures for everyone to participate.

- Massively multiplayer games, such as *World of Warcraft*, can contain any of the structures just described. Individuals are very free to play at any level of engagement that's appropriate for them, and they can go through phases of greater and lesser participation.

Location

Where will players physically be located relative to one another, and how will their proximity affect the gameplay?

Shared Space

A shared physical space like a living room has important implications for play, because much of the experience will happen outside the borders of the game world. When people play together in a shared space, they taunt one another, joke around, high-five, obstruct each other's view, yell, scream, and cheer. Meaningful moments in the game are magnified, as when one player suddenly leaps ahead of another or makes a mistake and ends up at a disadvantage. The more of these moments the game offers, the greater the effect it will have in a shared space.

Also think about how the game's display will support multiple players in a single space. Sharing a computer screen and playing "pass the mouse" makes for a pretty lousy experience. Instead, is it feasible for all players to have their own display, perhaps using multiple laptops or mobile devices? Would players share a split screen, or would the game's display allow multiple players to use the same screen at the same time? How would that work, and how would individual players be able to tell what they personally were affecting?

Remote Play

Since the late 1990s, more and more people have experienced video games through online play. The online environment removes a lot of ambiguity from game design because players have their own display and controls. It can also be very convenient for players because they don't need to jump into a car and drive across town to play a game with their friends. Players miss out on the nonverbal language and rich personal interaction of a shared space, but the convenience of remote play also means that more people can play together more often.

Timing

Will players be able to interact with one another in real time?

Synchronous Multiplayer

In online games like *Unreal* and *World of Warcraft*, players interact in real time. Real-time interaction allows events to develop quickly, lets players react to one another's actions immediately, and enables a large number of player-to-player interactions at any given time. These interactions are very conversational, contributing to the players' feeling that they're participating in an active community. However, real-time interaction works only if many players are logged in at the same time, so synchronous multiplayer games lend themselves to configurations that maximize the number of players available at any particular time. This may mean allowing lots of players to participate at once, or allowing strangers to interact with one another.

Asynchronous Multiplayer

In some games, players make their respective contributions to the game asynchronously, taking actions as their time allows. Their moves are then stored on a central server until other players can go in and check them, also at their own convenience. Asynchronous play has the great advantage of not requiring players to schedule time to play together, and it lends itself to play among small circles of friends. Interactions between players must be fairly simple and involve small numbers of moves; asynchronous play doesn't work well for fighting pitched battles or for anything that unfolds in the moment.

Familiarity

Will players already be known to one another outside of the game?

Friend-Based Association

Many players feel more comfortable playing a game with people they know. You may prefer to allow people to play only with friends from work, school, Facebook, or their personal address books, especially if some players could be children.

Open Association

A large number of highly successful commercial games pair players with complete strangers online. For many players, the opportunity to meet new people through a game is a major part of the appeal of online play. Furthermore, allowing open association broadens the pool of potential players immensely, making it much more likely that enough people are in the game at any one time to sustain the experience. Concerns about safety can be mitigated if people have limited means of direct communication with one another as in *Club Penguin*, Disney's virtual community for kids, which allows players to communicate only through canned phrases (Figure 6.3).

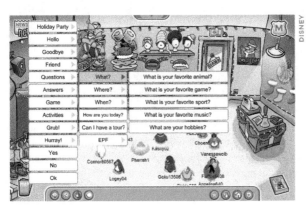

FIGURE 6.3
Players in *Club Penguin* can interact with one another only by selecting canned phrases from a list.

Stance

How do you want players to relate to one another in the game?

Competitive

Competitive games drive everyone toward greater skill and effort, and they encourage players to size up one another's strategies. Players need to dive into one another's psychology and exploit the weaknesses they believe they have identified there. They keep secrets, bluff, obfuscate, hide, and otherwise employ trickery to win. Think about whether these qualities would complement the design of your game.

In some contexts (for example, a workplace or charitable organization), you might assume that putting players in a competitive stance would be thematically unpalatable. But keep in mind that the shared experience of play tends to bring people together.

Cooperative

Cooperative play creates a very different kind of experience. To succeed, players must build a relational culture between one another that is based on how they can work together. Doing this means understanding each other's skills, developing a shared set of dependable routines, and creating a specialized vocabulary for communicating within the game. By living the practice of sharing, trusting, aiding, and leading, cooperative games can generate strong bonds between players.

Neutral

In some games, players neither compete against nor cooperate with one another, but are merely present in the game at the same time. In *Animal Crossing*, for example, players can visit one another's cities, see how they've decorated their houses, and leave messages for one another (Figure 6.4). The point of the multiplayer model here is to facilitate a social experience and foster a sense of community, not to advance the gameplay.

Hybrid

It can be fun to have both cooperative and competitive stances between players. In *Team Fortress 2*, players operate cooperatively on either the red team or the blue team, and the two teams compete against each other in battle. In a clever twist on these stances, players may take on the role of a spy and disguise themselves as members of the opposing team (Figure 6.5). Enemy medics may actually be tricked into healing a spy, who is only there to wreak havoc on the enemy team.

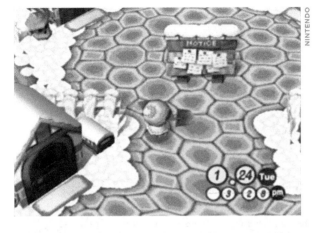

FIGURE 6.4
Players can post messages for one another in *Animal Crossing.* Although they're aware of one another's presence, the players neither cooperate nor compete.

FIGURE 6.5
A spy disguises himself as a member of the enemy team in *Team Fortress 2.* To players on the opposing team, he appears as the character on his mask.

Roles and Power

Will all players stand on an equal footing in the game?

Symmetrical

In most games, players start out with roughly equivalent amounts of power. This balance gives a game a sense of fairness and makes it an unbiased arbiter of who has the greater skill. Battleship, chess, and *Pong* are examples of games in which the assigned roles of the players and the power they have are completely symmetrical.

Not all games need to specify the same role for all players, or grant them the same amount of power. Hangman is an asymmetrical game, for example, because the two people play completely different roles. In *Dungeons & Dragons*, one player serves as the dungeon master and the other players are the denizens of the dungeon master's world. Baseball has many asymmetrical elements, as when the batter faces off against nine other players, each of whom has a very different role on the field.

Genre

Considering how the established game genres could support your objectives can be a helpful way to generate design concepts. Each genre has distinct characteristics that lend themselves to particular modes of play and engagement, which in turn create different advantages for design. For example, the complex and cognitively demanding character of strategy games could work well for a game intended to educate players about the basic principles of natural selection.

Table 6.1 lists game genres that may be relevant to designs intended to achieve broader objectives in the real world. Select several from the list, and ask yourself how each might suit your objective and the motivations of your target audience. Can you visualize the game through the lens of that genre? Keep in mind, too, that one of the most exciting attributes of video games is that they often transcend genre and reinvent traditional forms of play. Games like *Katamari Damacy* and *Angry Birds* have been very successful doing things that had never been done before. Wonderful things can happen when you mash different genres together or explore the gaps that lie between them.

Putting It All Together

Throughout this chapter, I've suggested several discrete questions that can spark different ideas for a game. You can make your brainstorming more productive by considering several of these factors at once, and by exploring the designs that could result when you juxtapose them in different ways. By focusing less on the quality of any individual idea and more on the total volume of ideas, you give yourself the advantage of selecting and combining the most promising ideas from many potential designs.[1]

Many of the game characteristics discussed in this chapter can be thought of as opposing values on a spectrum. You can generate concepts by imagining what shape the game would take at each end of these spectra.

---

1 This section is heavily influenced by Leah Buley's discussion of generative design methods. Expect to see it covered in greater detail in her book *UX Team of One*, due out from Rosenfeld Media in 2012 (rosenfeldmedia.com/books/ux-team-of-one).

TABLE 6.1

GAME GENRES COMPARED		
Genre	Characteristics	Examples
Platformer	Reflexive Light narrative Lengthy	*LittleBigPlanet* *Ratchet & Clank* *Super Mario Bros.*
Role-playing games	Strategic and reflexive Deep narrative Very lengthy	*Final Fantasy* *Mass Effect* *World of Warcraft*
Action/arcade	Reflexive Fast-paced Usually short	*Galaga* *Geometry Wars* *Pac-Man*
Strategy	Strategic and tactical Complex Cognitively demanding	*Age of Empires* *Plants vs. Zombies* *Total War*
First-person shooter	Reflexive Intense Cathartic	*Call of Duty* *Halo* *Resistance*
Puzzle	Toylike Cognitively demanding Usually short	*Bejeweled* *Bust-a-Move* *Tetris*
Open world	Self-paced Invites exploration Lengthy	*Grand Theft Auto* *Infamous* *L.A. Noire*
Rhythm	Reflexive Often physical Short	*Dance Dance Revolution* *Guitar Hero* *Rock Band*
Simulation	Semblance of realism Invites experimentation Invites creativity	*FarmVille* *SimCity* *The Sims*
Virtual pet	Endearing Invites creativity Lengthy	*Animal Crossing* *EyePet* *Nintendogs*
Exergames	Physical Goal-oriented Somewhat short	*EA Sports Active* *Wii Fit* *Your Shape: Fitness Evolved*
Adventure	Cognitive Invites exploration Atmospheric	*King's Quest* *Myst* *Zork*
Brain games	Cognitive Goal-oriented Repetitive	*Big Brain Academy* *Brain Age* *Lumosity*
Social networking games	Communal Continual Viral	*CityVille* *Empires & Allies* *Words With Friends*
Alternate reality games	Linked to real life Multimedia Collective	*The Beast* *I Love Bees* *Why So Serious*

General Characteristics

- Win/lose versus open-ended
- Single player versus multiplayer
- Short duration versus long duration
- Single path versus multiple paths
- Realistic versus abstract

Conflict Characteristics

- Luck versus skill
- Reflexive versus strategic
- Virtual versus physical
- Experimental versus precise
- Creative versus destructive

Multiplayer Characteristics

- Cooperative versus competitive
- Synchronous versus asynchronous
- Shared space versus remote
- Symmetrical roles versus asymmetrical roles
- Friend-based versus open association

For example, suppose that your objective is to teach tenth-graders basic physics and you choose to generate concepts using the "single path versus multiple paths" spectrum (Figure 6.6). At the single path end, the result might be a puzzle game based on miniature golf in which the player always needs to get a hole in one, and for each hole the player must determine the correct angle of the putt and the amount of force to apply to successfully get the ball through the obstacles.

At the multiple paths end of the spectrum, you might imagine a simulation game in which players construct solar systems from an interstellar cloud by creating gravity wells into which gases and rubble may coalesce into stars and planets. The objective might be to end up with at least one planet orbiting at a distance from a star where it would be hospitable to the formation of life.

Objective: Teach basic physics

mini-golf game: must figure out the right angle and force to apply to get a hole in 1	solar system sim: manipulate gravity to create at least 1 planet in star's habitable zone
Single path	Multiple paths

FIGURE 6.6

Considering how a game would be designed at opposite ends of a spectrum can spark ideas for design.

After generating as many ideas for games as you can using one spectrum, move on to another one. What games can you envision that would require players to take reflexive actions in the moment, or to think through long-term strategic decisions in advance? What shape would the game take as a single-player experience versus a multiplayer experience? If the game were multiplayer, how might it work if the players went head-to-head in synchronous play or if they took turns asynchronously?

Another productive way to experiment with spectra is to take two at a time and put them in a 2×2 grid that gives you four quadrants representing different combinations of characteristics around which you can brainstorm ideas.

If you want to create a game based on physics, for example, you might use the grid to come up with the four ideas illustrated in Figure 6.7:

- **Creative/cooperative.** All players need to work together to figure out how to complete a partial course of virtual dominoes to be knocked down. At some points they need to make a domino swing across a rope or set off a cannon to propel a domino across the course.

- **Creative/competitive.** Each player needs to build a ship from dozens of interchangeable parts, each of which has some positive attributes, like thrust and buoyancy, as well as negative attributes, like weight and drag. Players then race their ships against one another.

- **Destructive/cooperative.** Two players need to launch rockets filled with debris to destroy asteroids of different masses hurtling toward the Earth, without running out of debris or fuel. One player is responsible for determining the mass of the debris for each launch; the other player is responsible for determining how much fuel to use to accelerate the debris.

- **Destructive/competitive.** Two players take turns trying to destroy one another's forts using catapults and trebuchets. Each one has objects of different masses to hurl at one another and must select the launch vehicle, its position, and the angle of each throw.

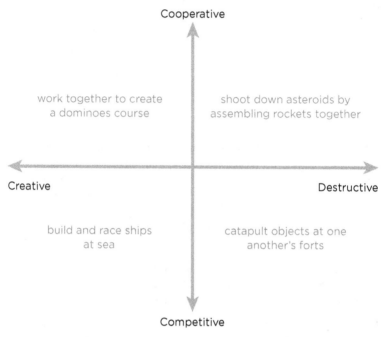

FIGURE 6.7
Using two spectra at once can give greater variation and richer detail to the ideas produced in a generative brainstorming session.

Keeping Your Priorities Straight

The methods I promote in this chapter will help you generate a variety of game concepts and then think through their designs. At some point you'll need to select the best ones to pursue. Remember that your first priority is to create a game that will provide a meaningful experience for its players. Your first question should be whether you believe the game will be fun, interesting, and rewarding to play, because these qualities will bear the greatest influence on the game's success.

CHAPTER 7

Creating Game
Prototypes

Once you have a solid concept for a game, you can start working out how you'll turn it into a playable experience. But development can be a risky venture. Games are inherently negotiated experiences; the designer normally just defines the parameters of play, within which the players bring the game to life. Part of the experience is created in advance, but the rest exists only in the moment of play. This means that it can be very difficult—if not impossible—to tell how well a game will play, short of actually playing it. You have to assume that the design of any game will go through a lot of revisions between conceptualization and launch.

It can also be very hard to think through all the fine points of a game's design right from the start. In particular, games that offer great depth of play and very involving experiences are necessarily complex undertakings. Game designers need reliable tools to help them refine an idea thoroughly and efficiently.

Prototyping meets both of these needs. It minimizes risk by exposing design problems early in the process. Designers can then focus on solutions that will improve the design. Prototyping also allows designers to flesh out and refine a game at a detailed level. It brings the gaps in the design into focus, and it's a cost-effective means by which designers can experiment with different ideas.

In this chapter I discuss two types of prototyping that will be familiar to UX designers, each of which has unique considerations in the context of game design. There's a natural progression between the methods, moving from lower to higher fidelity and ultimately to the final form of the game.

Practice with applying these methods to game design may even yield insight into better practices for the design of conventional user interfaces. I've often found that the shift in thinking that is required for designing games can crack open new approaches to UX design.

Paper Prototypes

Paper prototyping is beloved in the UX design community for its ability to support highly informative appraisals of early design concepts without the overhead of lengthy, expensive development cycles. But at first glance, this method we know so well might seem ill suited to many video games. Can you really represent the experience of a game like *Asteroids* on paper? It's difficult enough to get a paper prototype of a Web form to reflect the way it will behave in the real world. How then can you re-create the mechanic of flying through open space and firing wildly at giant boulders that crumble into smaller pieces shooting out in different directions, all while following Newtonian physics?

Stone Librande, creative director at Maxis, advocates using paper prototypes broadly in the design of video games. He challenges participants in his workshops to create paper versions of real games they've played in the past, and as it happens, one session actually produced an entirely offline version of *Asteroids* (Figure 7.1).

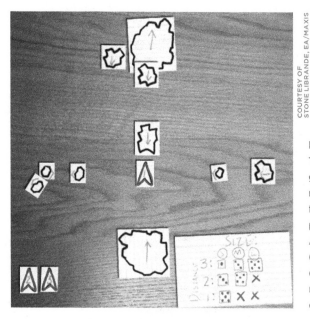

COURTESY OF
STONE LIBRANDE, EA/MAXIS

FIGURE 7.1
The classic arcade game *Asteroids*, re-created as a fully playable paper prototype. A probability matrix (bottom right) determines, from a die roll, whether a shot hit or missed.

In this simulation, players chose one of four directions in which to point their spaceship, from which asteroids approached one step on each turn. Players then rolled a die to fire, and a probability matrix based on the size of the asteroid and their distance from it determined whether they were successful. This prototype successfully reduced the game to its most basic interaction.

So at least some elements of video games are suited to paper prototyping. Even if some parts of a game you're working on don't translate, chances are that other parts do. That's okay; you don't have to re-create the game as a whole faithfully. But wherever an opportunity exists to answer a design question on paper, the expediency and affordability of the paper method make it worthwhile.

What Works on Paper?

While paper prototypes usually can't offer a precise representation of an entire game experience, there are some common aspects of a game's design that they are especially good at evaluating.

Balance

Paper is a great tool for efficiently figuring out which values to assign to elements in the game so that they balance well against one another. See the sidebar for an example of how Stone Librande applied paper prototypes toward this end in the design of *Spore*.

Stone Librande

The video game *Spore* (EA/Maxis, 2008) is an epic spanning the evolution of life on a planet. The player begins the game controlling a primitive organism in a small tide pool. Over time the organism evolves into a sentient race of creatures that, if successful, will conquer the planet and eventually colonize the galaxy.

I was the lead designer on the first portion of *Spore*, called the "Cell Game." In this stage of the game the player starts out as a weak tadpole-like creature. The player's goal is to navigate through increasingly hostile waters and crawl up onto land. To accomplish this, the player must make the creature evolve by growing new parts in response to environmental challenges.

One of my first tasks on this project was to determine what these parts were and how they affected the player's experience. It was easy to generate long lists of interesting animal parts, but this was the beginning of the game and we did not want to overwhelm the player. My design challenge was to efficiently pick the smallest number of parts

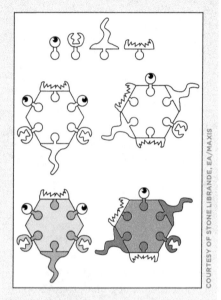

FIGURE 7.2

A simple model for cell creatures allowing different body parts to be snapped on. Each part had its own attributes and abilities, and the prototype helped balance them against one another.

while still providing the greatest amount of gameplay variance. Instead of jumping right in and building an electronic prototype (which would have required the assistance of a programmer and an artist), I decided to test the initial ideas by making a simple board game. This was not intended to be an exact representation of the PC game experience, but only a quick way to determine how many parts we needed, what the special abilities were going to be, and how the different parts should relate to one another in terms of power.

Using index cards, scissors, tape, and paper clips, I mocked up a crude collection of creature parts (Figure 7.2). Players could make different creatures by choosing which of these parts they wanted to attach to its central body. Did you want to try a speed strategy? Add more fins. Or maybe you wanted to concentrate on offensive abilities? Add powerful jaws. How about taking it slow and steady with lots of armor? Add some spikes. By simply hooking together different parts in different combinations, a player could make hundreds of unique creatures.

Next I printed out a large hex grid for the board. The goal of this game was to move your creature around the grid and collect colored beads ("food") that were placed randomly in the hexes. Players would "swim" around the board in an attempt to gather the most food without dying.

Using the prototype, I was able to do most of the early testing by myself. I would have my mutant creatures fight each other to determine which "build" would be the best (Figure 7.3). If a particular strategy dominated the tide pool, then the corresponding parts were weakened (or removed from the game entirely), while other parts were strengthened. After a few play sessions I had generated a list of potential parts, the associated abilities (electric zap, poison spray, blood-sucking proboscis, and so on), and the tuning parameters that could be tweaked to make each part weaker or stronger.

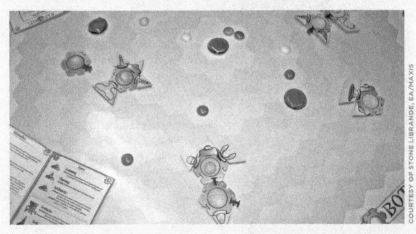

COURTESY OF STONE LIBRANDE, EA/MAXIS

FIGURE 7.3

The cell game prototype developed for *Spore* was so robust that it could be run as its own fully playable board game.

By working out the design as a paper prototype, I was able to save weeks of programming and art time. The final list contained just nine parts but covered the most important aspects of gameplay (movement, combat, and eating) while giving the player freedom to experiment and customize. Although there was still a lot of work to do to turn these ideas into a playable real-time PC game, the part list in the final shipping product is the same as the one that was determined while working on the paper prototype.

Stone Librande is the creative director at EA/Maxis and teaches game design at Cogswell College in Sunnyvale, California. He is a regular speaker at the annual Game Developers Conference, where he runs a workshop on paper-prototyping game ideas.

CYAN WORLDS

FIGURE 7.4
The flooded-lighthouse puzzle from *Myst*. The player needs to get a locked chest to float to the position where a key can reach it.

Rules

You can think of a game as a system in which events play themselves out according to the set of rules you create. Different rules result in different player behaviors, outcomes, and durations of play. How many moves should a player be able to make in one turn? How often should players be allowed to execute a special move? Should two players be allowed to occupy the same space at one time? You can use paper prototyping to experiment with different rule sets and see what effects they have. Run the prototype game repeatedly, altering the rules in each iteration while keeping all other factors the same.

Puzzles

Some puzzles, such as the pattern-matching mechanic of *Bejeweled*, can be directly translated to a paper prototype. Other puzzles can be abstracted to a point where their basic challenge is fully represented on paper. For example, one challenge in *Myst* involves pumping water from one flooded area to another to allow access to different puzzle elements (Figure 7.4). Players need to figure out the correct sequence in which to open up a room and make use of its components. At one point, the player must drain water from a chest and then seal it shut so that it will float when the room is flooded again.

Although the full game involves traversing an elaborately detailed ship several times and operating realistically rusty machinery, the puzzle underlying that graphical presentation is just a set of on/off conditions. This basic mechanic can be modeled using index cards to describe the state of each component, and a flowchart to determine which outcomes follow particular conditions (Figure 7.5). Creating a puzzle like this on paper is a great way to develop the basic puzzle design and discover how people respond to it.

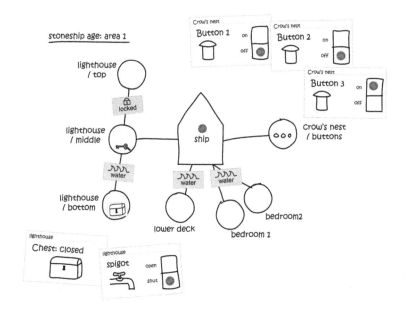

Stoneship age: Area 1

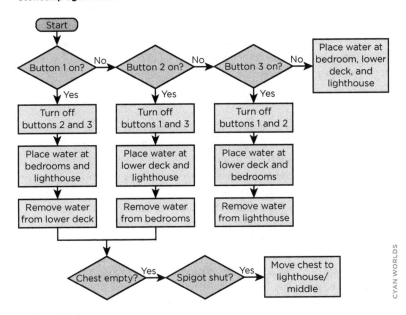

FIGURE 7.5
Complex puzzles can be quickly and cheaply designed and tested on paper using a few index cards, maps, and flowcharts.

The environment in which the game is played can also often be prototyped on paper. Paper-prototyping the environment can help to establish how different spaces are related, how far players need to travel, what strategies the environmental constraints allow, and so on. Suppose you're developing a role-playing game in which players periodically have battlefield encounters. The progress of each battle may be heavily influenced by different elements in the environment. It may, for example, contain rivers that can be crossed only by winged characters, or rocks that allow characters to attack with projectiles from behind cover. Running the game on a paper prototype can help you design maps that produce better gameplay. You can even model 3D environments by breaking out the Legos.

Building a Paper Prototype

Strip the Gameplay Down to Its Core

It's natural to think of video games as rich experiences full of audiovisual splendor. But at their core, they consist of fundamental conflicts that players are trying to resolve. For the sake of a paper prototype, you want to disregard all of the accoutrements of the interface and focus on the underlying mechanic of play. Pennies work well as character tokens, and index cards can be used for character properties, actions, or objects. This is about all you need to prototype the battle system of a role-playing game like *Final Fantasy VII* sufficiently to build a basic set of attacks, defenses, magic spells, and summoned monsters and test them against different enemies.

Don't Be Too Literal

Don't try to model the actual experience of the finished game in a paper prototype. Complete video games, with their real-time action and manifold interactions, are usually too complex to translate onto paper. Instead, focus each prototype on an elemental piece of the game for which it's important to get the design right. Notice that the *Asteroids* prototype I described earlier didn't have the spaceship actually flying through space; it didn't need to, because it was just good enough to provide useful insight into the shooting mechanic. Focus on what will be sufficient to answer your design question, and don't worry too much about other aspects of how the game will work. If needed, you can always create additional prototypes to examine other aspects of the gameplay.

Minimize Bookkeeping and Computation

The more fluidly a paper prototype executes, the more insight you can get out of it in a given period of time. You don't want to get bogged down in excessive bookkeeping to continually note the condition of each spaceship in a fleet, or in excessive computation to calculate the amount of fuel each ship consumes, given its mass. Those may be great elements to have in the finished game, but don't overcomplicate the prototype by trying to model them on paper.

Instead, group things that have related attributes into a single entity in the prototype, and then act on their aggregated value. For example, instead of calculating the mass of individual spaceships, you could use coins to represent each cargo item a ship holds, so that the data is easy to visualize and maintain. Eliminate as much math as you can from the prototype.

Replace Skill with Probability

Clearly, jumping, shooting, and dodging attacks can't work the same way on paper as they do on-screen. But they don't necessarily need to. Instead, you can substitute probability for many of the skill-based components of games.

Suppose you're modeling a battle sequence in *Halo* on paper. In the actual game, players have a greater probability of getting a kill using the sniper rifle than they do with a low-precision weapon like the plasma pistol. Equivalently, players expend more ammunition using the pistol. To prototype the battle, first invest $5 in a set of polyhedral dice. Then create an index card for each enemy, assign a die to each weapon, and note the number that players need to roll to score a kill. To kill a grunt, one of the weaker enemies, players may need to roll a 1 or 2 on a 6-sided die using the sniper rifle (a 66 percent chance) or a 5 or lower on a 20-sided die using the pistol (a 25 percent chance); otherwise the enemy scores a hit on the player. If the player gets the kill, then the number rolled could represent the amount of ammunition used in the effort. This setup would allow you to experiment with factors like the number and types of enemies that players face, the number of those enemies that are behind cover, and the amount of ammunition and health available to the player.

If you want to get a feel for how this works in practice, pick up a set of Strat-O-Matic baseball cards online or at a hobby shop (Figure 7.6). Together with a set of dice, these cards allow you to build fantasy teams of real-life players and simulate baseball games using their real-world statistics from a specific season. While Strat-O-Matic games may be very low tech, they effectively represent the rules and basic gameplay that lie at the core of baseball.

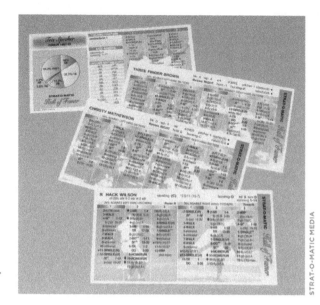

FIGURE 7.6
Strat-O-Matic allows
players to simulate
the core gameplay
underlying baseball
using real-world player
statistics.

Make It a Real Game

A prototype works especially well when it has a set of objectives, environmental constraints, and formal constraints that make it a complete (if small) game unto itself. Consider making it a game in which two people face off as opponents, even if you're developing a one-player game. Playing the prototype as a real game helps generate insights because it focuses attention on the game's fundamental conflict. It enables the people testing the game to more accurately assess whether it's too easy or too difficult, because they're really trying to outdo one another. Used in this way, a paper prototype stands a better chance of exposing holes in the design.

In the best circumstances you might even find that the paper game itself is pretty fun to play. A good game is a good game, regardless of the medium on which it's played.

Iterate

Finally, treat the prototype as a generative design tool and iterate it several times. This is the best time to do it, since paper is so cheap and easy to work with. Get together with a group to test-drive the prototype. Once you begin playing, people will start to come up with new ideas. Keep plenty of pens and index cards handy to capture their ideas, and then experiment with adding those suggestions to the design. Discard anything that isn't working, and continue refining the flow until it feels appropriately challenging and fun.

Electronic Prototypes

Working on paper can get you only so far. At some point you need to investigate aspects of the design that can't be sufficiently represented on paper, such as the pace of gameplay, the way online players will interact with one another, or whether people will feel comfortable with the control scheme. To get a sense of what it actually feels like to play it, you need to introduce the complexity that the computational and data-intensive elements will bring to the live game. At this point, it's time to start developing electronic prototypes of the game.

Building an Electronic Prototype

Prepare Research Questions before Deciding What to Prototype

Prototypes fulfill specific purposes in the development of a game. The more questions that a single prototype can address, the more useful it will be. In the process of documenting the idea for a game, periodically take a step back and think about areas where you're not precisely sure how the gameplay should work, concepts that feel like they might be on the wrong track, or things that could potentially go wrong if your assumptions don't hold up. Be critical (remember, this is all for the sake of reducing risk), and write your questions down so that you'll have them when you're building the prototypes. Here are some examples of questions you might prepare:

- How quickly should enemy characters move?

- How should the targeting system work?

- Will people get through the challenges too quickly?

- Is the process of creating a new character too cumbersome and time-consuming?

- Can players complete this challenge in any way that bypasses the intended solution?

With these research questions in hand, you'll be better able to decide what should go into the prototype. You may well be coding something that represents several disjointed parts from the overall game. That's okay as long as you're learning something valuable from each part.

Start as Small as You Can

Don't prototype anything more than you need to. It's easy to bite off too much and spend too much time developing prototypes. Remember that prototyping should be done rapidly, so that you can implement the necessary changes and make a new prototype.

Start with the elements that represent the core mechanic of the game to see how well they're working. Such an element might be just a character jumping from one ledge to another, a farm with only one plant for you to grow, or a single set of turns taken by each player. It's important to get the low-level elements of the design right first, because they generalize to the game experience as a whole. If they work in the prototype, you'll be more confident that they'll work in their proper context.

Work from Wireframes

As in UX design, a good set of well-annotated wireframes can save a lot of time in the design of games by clearly specifying what needs to be prototyped and ensuring that the coded delivery is faithful to the intended vision (Figure 7.7). With a reliable set of wireframes, developers can concentrate on building the prototype and work more independently, without having to worry about having to revise the code again and again. All of this helps to keep cycle times short and development costs low.

Wireframes are also a great tool for talking about the design with other members of the team. Graphic designers have a basis for creating image assets. Developers can generate estimates of work. Business sponsors get a sense of the game's direction. Everyone starts to develop a shared vocabulary for critically discussing the game.

Don't Overdesign

Especially in the early stages, your prototypes can be as ugly as they need to be. Visual design is an important element of games, but artwork can't sustain the experience without a foundation of high-quality gameplay. First and foremost, you should be concerned with whether the game itself is inherently interesting, challenging, and fun. Cut out excessive animations. Cut out backgrounds. Cut out lighting effects. Cut out color. Cut out sound. Cut, cut, cut. There will be time to add all of this later. Focus instead on the things that make the game worth playing.

Squeeze as Much Use Out of a Prototype as You Can

Because electronic prototypes are relatively costly to build, you want to get every bit of life out of them that you can. As you improve the prototype and gain confidence in its design, continue building off of it. Keep making incremental enhancements as you go, incorporating progressively larger parts of the game experience. Bring the prototype into playtesting (described in the next chapter) and solicit player feedback on the design. Move gradually toward greater fidelity, incorporating image assets and sounds as they become available. In the best case, you'll be able to reuse much of this code in developing the game itself.

Putting

Setting putt direction

States of the direction arrow

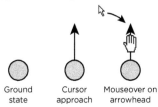

Ground   Cursor   Mouseover on
state   approach   arrowhead

The direction arrow occurs in three states:

• When the mouse cursor is distant from the ball, the direction arrow does not occur.

• As the mouse approaches the ball, the direction arrow appears.

• When the player rolls over the arrowhead, the cursor changes to a "grab" symbol.

Initiating a putt

Mouseover state	Mousedown state

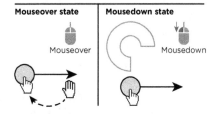

Mouseover   Mousedown

When the player rolls over the golf ball, the pointer changes to a "click" symbol.

When the mouse button is pressed down, the putt is initiated.

The force meter appears in an area proximal to the

Moving the direction arrow

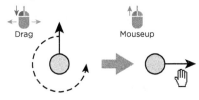

Drag   Mouseup

The player may click and drag the arrowhead to set the direction of the putt.

The arrow can be dragged 360 degrees around the golf ball. When the mouse button is released, the direction is set.

The direction may be reset by clicking and dragging the arrow again.

Executing a putt

Setting force	Hitting the ball

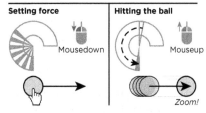

Mousedown   Mouseup

Zoom!

As the player holds the mouse button down, the force meter continues to build to its maximum value.

When the player releases the mouse button, the force meter quickly returns to zero and the ball is hit with the specified amount of force.

UNISYS

FIGURE 7.7

Effective wireframing is an invaluable skill in game design. A portion of a wireframe from a mini-golf game is shown here.

Don't let the act of creating a prototype overcommit you to a design that isn't working. Games don't always work as well in practice as they do in theory. You may discover that the vision you had for the gameplay experience just doesn't materialize, and the prototype may reveal that the game isn't any fun to play. You don't have to give up; you may find ways to make the design work by iterating the prototype. But you also might need to go back and pursue a radically different design. If you've been following the advice in this chapter, then this realization should come at the earliest possible moment and with the fewest downsides. Go ahead and ball it up, take a breath, and then give it another go.

Prototyping Saves Time and Money (Really!)

When you've got a solid idea and feel really excited about it, prototyping can seem like a waste of time. It can be very tempting to jump as quickly as possible from concept to all-out development. But doing so is ultimately self-defeating, because it will inevitably lead to more revisions to the finished code—when such changes are most expensive. Adopting a disciplined process that moves from low-fidelity prototypes to higher-fidelity ones over the course of the design cycle will result in better games produced at lower cost.

Prototyping is a great way to minimize the risk inherent in a game design project of any complexity. To get the most out of prototypes, you need reliable methods of assessing the quality of the gameplay experience. In the next chapter I'll discuss how to test your designs.

CHAPTER 8

Playtesting

It's difficult to overstate the importance of testing in the context of game design. Because games are highly dynamic systems, any number of outcomes can emerge when real people with different skills, experiences, and expectations sit down and play. Just as UX designers benefit by seeing what happens when people actually use their interfaces, game designers benefit by seeing what happens when people actually play their games. Testing early and often sets up a cycle in which testing informs game design, which generates improvements to the experience, which in turn need to be tested. In his influential book *The Art of Game Design*, Jesse Schell goes so far as to say that "good games are created through playtesting."[1]

Playtesting encompasses all of the same objectives as usability testing, as well as many more. In fact, it serves so many objectives that it constitutes a distinct practice. In playtesting, you're weighing design elements that seldom are concerns in conventional usability, such as:

- How much fun players have.
- Which parts of the game are too difficult or too easy.
- How long people feel motivated to play before they become bored.
- Whether the amount of experience required to level up is appropriate.
- Whether the strengths of different skills are balanced against one another.
- Whether people find the story line interesting, amusing, or heart-wrenching.
- Whether players identify with the characters in the game.

Still, playtesting proceeds in much the same way as the good old usability testing we all know and love. That is, it is best handled as frequently scheduled one-on-one sessions with participants who are asked to think aloud as they complete a set of objectives while a facilitator records observations about their actions. UX designers should feel very much at home in such playtests and find that their existing skills translate quite well. For this reason, I won't dwell on the basic procedures and logistics of playtesting, but instead on the considerations that are specific to games.

Classes of Problems

In playtesting, designers need to look for a very broad set of potential problems. These include:

- **Usability.** As we all know, usability is the extent to which players understand the interface and are able to successfully operate it to achieve intended tasks.

---

1 Schell, J. (2008). *The art of game design*. Burlington, MA: Morgan Kaufmann, p. 389.

- **Ergonomics.** Often a concern of conventional testing, ergonomics is especially important in games, because each has its own custom mapping of controls. You may find that the placement of the buttons assigned to aiming and firing makes it too difficult for players to do both at the same time, for example.

- **Aesthetics.** In addition to the visual and aural design of the game, aesthetics includes the storytelling elements of narrative and character development, the tactile experience of vibrating and force feedback controllers, and the game's sense of humor. Testing is a great opportunity to see whether the jokes fall flat or people think the story is pretentious.

- **Agility.** How much physical skill the game demands of the player to succeed. Testers need to consider questions like whether a jump is too difficult for players to time correctly, or whether too many enemies are firing on the player at once.

- **Balance.** The attributes assigned to the different elements in the game must work in combination to create an experience that's seen as fair and equitable.

- **Puzzles.** Players must be able to solve the cognitive challenges that the game presents. For each puzzle encountered, are most people able to "get it" with the right amount of applied thought, or do they tend to become irrevocably stumped?

- **Motivation.** Players should perceive the rewards of playing as sufficient to continue trying. Do players take an active interest in the game? If so, how long is it sustained? At what point do people lose interest, and why? Would they be better motivated by different rewards or game structures?

- **Affect.** Most important, playtesting needs to examine whether players have positive feelings about the experience. When they're playing, are they enjoying themselves? Are they bored, frustrated, or amused? After playing, do they regard the experience as time well spent? Do they want to continue playing the game after the playtest is over?

General Guidelines

Many of the guidelines discussed in this section apply to usability testing as well, but they take on a pronounced importance in the context of playtesting.

Recruit Selectively

Because games are meant to be enjoyable experiences, a large number of people are wonderfully enthusiastic about participating in playtesting. Although these players are a great resource, keep in mind that they might not play the same way other important elements of your target audience would play. Recruiting exclusively from eager volunteers may result in oversampling players who are disproportionately skilled, knowledgeable, or positively biased toward gaming. Such a misrepresentative sample can distort the picture of the game that emerges from testing.

In particular, many of the applications of game design discussed in this book are targeted at traditional gamers and nongamers alike. Make a concerted effort to recruit test participants who represent the diversity of your actual target audience. Be sure to sample among genders, ages, ethnicities, income levels, education levels, and game aptitudes in proportion to the communities in which you'll be promoting the game. If you're targeting a very specific gamer demographic (for example, unmarried 24- to 30-year-old female college graduates living in urban areas and working in finance), focus on just those people. Write up a set of screener questions to probe for these criteria, and conduct phone interviews before accepting participants into the test. If you can't get the participants you need from volunteers alone, consider enlisting the help of an agency.

Emulate the Play Environment to the Best of Your Ability

Lab-based testing always has the disadvantage of creating an artificial environment that can alter the way people behave in the real world. The testing environment is particularly a concern for playtesting, because players would normally feel very much at ease while gaming. Seating them in a testing lab in front of one-way glass from which muffled comments and chuckles occasionally emanate can completely kill the experience.

Whenever possible, use remote testing and screen-sharing software to observe players using the game on their home or work computers. This method has a lot of appeal, because players are in the environment where they would normally experience the game anyway. Be sure to ask players about the location from which they're remoting so that you can better understand the way they would typically play your game. See Nate Bolt and Tony Tulathimutte's book *Remote Research* for an in-depth guide to running tests long-distance.[2]

Remote testing is not always feasible, though, especially if you're developing for a platform other than a desktop computer. When you must do lab-based testing, do it in a location that resembles the conditions in which players actually play. Let them sprawl out on a couch, a recliner, or a beanbag chair. Banish fluorescent lighting. Paint the walls in colors other than white or gray. Offer them a beer (laws permitting). Show them where the restroom is, and invite them to take a break whenever they feel the urge. Make it feel cozy (Figure 8.1).

---

2   Bolt, N., & Tulathimutte, T. (2010). *Remote research: Real users, real time, real research.* New York, NY: Rosenfeld Media (rosenfeldmedia.com/books/remote-research).

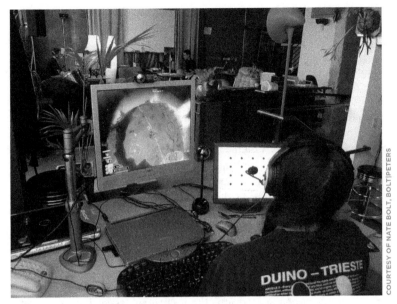

FIGURE 8.1
Consulting company Bolt | Peters provides a comfortable space for playtesting—a sharp contrast to the conventionally stuffy usability lab.

Sit Back and Stay Quiet

The question-and-answer style of facilitation that's the norm in usability testing is too intrusive for playtesting. Players need time to focus and enter a state of flow, and there's a significant risk that your questions will influence their behavior in the game. It may take some practice, but get used to sitting back and observing quietly. Provide minimal direction, and avoid asking questions unless you really need to. You'll get less benefit from the think-aloud protocol as players turn their attention to the gameplay, but that's okay, because players need time to concentrate on what they're doing. You might break in at the worst possible moment to interrupt, and lose a chance to gain valuable insight. Let it go and wait until the next break, and then just remind the players again to try to think out loud. Take careful notes while the test is in progress, and discuss your observations with the players after they're done.

Prepare an Observation Script

Instead of the traditional test script, prepare a script of key events that you especially want to observe people handling. Get ready for the test by running through the game and making note of the points around which the play turns—for example, when the player needs to learn a new skill, when a hint to the solution of a puzzle is dropped, or when a tougher enemy is first introduced. Draw up a list of these events and spend some time studying it (they might happen in any order). As each event arises in the game, note the players' level of success in the situation, their apparent understanding of what's happening, and their subsequent action in the game.

Go Long

Usability tests of conventional user interfaces seldom last longer than two hours, which is more than sufficient when a user's typical interaction with a website lasts only a few minutes. But depending on the design, video games can run quite long. Many of the most important observations that testing can provide might not become apparent until the player is hours into the experience. On the other hand, the quality of feedback will start to diminish after a few hours, so all-day sessions aren't the way to go either.

If you're testing a long game, break the evaluation into multiple sessions of two to three hours each. That'll provide enough time per sitting for people to get comfortable with the game without becoming overly fatigued. If confidentiality concerns permit, even consider allowing players to continue playing the game on their own after the observation session is done, so that they can e-mail you with additional thoughts. Extended testing outside of the formal testing environment can be an invaluable way to evaluate engagement with the game over the long term.

Stay Flexible

Early in development, you may find that the prototypes you're testing are plagued with problems—bugs, glitches, and challenges that you never imagined a player would have. In the test, be ready to skip to a completely different track as needed to get past something that just isn't working. If you have more tests lined up, make sure the development team is on call to start working on any problems that are exposed in the course of testing, so that you can get the most out of the next session.

Distinguishing Real Problems from Appropriate Challenges

In traditional UX design, the ideal is for every task to be completed with as little difficulty as possible. This is not equally true of game design, because an appropriate level of challenge is an important part of the experience. If a game demands too little, it can fail to hold the player's interest. At the same time, it's important to identify real problems that unnecessarily diminish the quality of the player experience.

Evaluating a game's difficulty correctly can be a real dilemma in playtesting, where it can be difficult to distinguish real problems from valuable challenges. People may express frustration with a portion of the game, but simply removing all sources of frustration would inevitably make the game less engaging. When you observe players having difficulty in a testing session, there are a few key questions you should ask yourself before deciding on a course of action.

Are Players Having a Hard Time for the Right Reasons?

First consider whether the source of the difficulty is the intended challenge of the design. Suppose a game contains a puzzle that requires players to slide tiles around a board to put them in order. If players are having difficulty getting the tiles to slide in the direction they intend, then they're spending time on the puzzle's interface rather than the cognitive challenge of the puzzle itself. UX designers will find that their background makes them adept at identifying such usability problems and synthesizing appropriate fixes.

In a more complex case, suppose that players aren't tripped up by the puzzle's interface but instead are having difficulty understanding what the puzzle requires them to do, or formulating the right strategy to complete it. These are arguably parts of the challenge of the puzzle itself and are not necessarily problems demanding resolution. Again, think about whether these challenges are intended parts of the design and whether the puzzle is more enjoyable because of them. If not, then more contextual help might be in order to help people focus on the real challenge. But if they are an intended part of the design, you'll need to consider some additional questions.

Do Players See the Challenge as Engaging or Discouraging?

Observe whether the problem is damaging to the player's willingness to keep at it. This question is tricky to evaluate, because a person's feelings of frustration may be only temporary. It's even common for players who feel stuck to get up and walk away for a while, only to come back and decide to give it another go. It's a good idea to allow players the latitude to do this in testing, rather than making them feel strapped to the chair.

When players make comments like "This is really tough," it's okay to ask them to clarify whether they mean it's good tough or bad tough. Be careful to stay neutral, though, and not to ask too many questions that might change the way your players would behave. You don't want to lead them toward a conclusion they wouldn't have drawn on their own.

As long as players show that they're motivated to keep trying of their own accord, it's a good sign that the challenge is engaging their interest and would be considered worthwhile. But if they truly throw in the towel, it's time to assess whether the design should be changed. Even if they don't completely give up, consider the cumulative effect of such experiences on players, and whether people are inclined to characterize the game as a whole as frustrating.

Is the Level of Challenge Appropriate for the Current Stage of the Game?

Ideally, games start out by accommodating players who have very little skill. As the game progresses, players are prepared for the incrementally higher challenge of the next stage by merit of having successfully mastered the previous one, and the game gradually becomes more demanding of their skill. Demand too much and the experience becomes frustrating; demand too little and the experience feels boring (Figure 8.2).

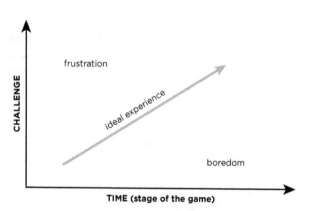

FIGURE 8.2
An ideal experience should offer a steadily increasing level of challenge over the course of the game, or else it risks becoming either too frustrating or too boring.

In this light, consider where the challenge presented to the player falls on what should be a smoothly ascending slope. If previous experience didn't provide sufficient practice for the current challenge, then players will be more likely to feel discouraged before they've given the game a real chance.

Super Mario Bros., for example, starts out by requiring players to master simple jumps and face off against enemies who don't have especially potent offensive capabilities. But by the end of the game, players are timing jumps to moving platforms while avoiding spurts of erupting lava and facing enemies that shoot fire and daggers. These feats can be difficult for any player, but they're a reasonable challenge for players who have had time to practice with each of the elements earlier in the game. The same challenges would be exclusionary if they came too early in the game, prompting more players to drop out in frustration. In testing, measure the appropriateness of a challenge by the number of players who are able to successfully clear it, the number of attempts at it, and the total time to completion.

What In-Game Actions Do Players Take in Response to the Challenge?

When trying to solve a problem, are people generally on the right track or do they attribute their difficulty to the wrong causes? Say, for example, that players need to find a key to open a door. Do they start looking for the key, or do they ignore the door and focus their attention on the useless window down the hall? People need to understand the nature of the problems they face and the actions that are available to them, and they must have a reasonable basis for figuring out what they need to do. They must be able to construct a mental model that contains the problem in order to create theories about how to solve it.

By paying attention to how players react when they're faced with a problem, you can get a sense of whether the design is what it should be. In the case of the door and the key, you might need to provide a stronger cue to direct players' attention to the door and to suggest that a key is available.

How Do Players Reflect on the Challenge after Surmounting It?

One of the best measures of a problem is how players feel about it once some time has passed since they overcame it. In retrospect, they may remember an experience that felt frustrating at the time as ultimately rewarding or as inconsequential in the broader context of the game.

Don't ask people to reflect on problems right away, when negative emotions are still fresh. Instead, keep a list of the problems people encounter as they play the game, and when the testing is over, ask them to recall their most positive and negative experiences of the game. Then prompt them to comment on specific problems they faced and how they feel about them now. Persistent negative feelings about those problems are a good sign that the design should be revisited.

Evaluating Motivation: The PENS Model

How can you assess whether most players will feel engaged by a game experience? You could set out to test for fun, but fun is a funny thing. It's very subjective and can be defined in any number of ways. It's hard to test for something so amorphous, because there are no good standards for saying what level of fun is sufficient or what type of fun players should be having.

A model that has gained a great deal of traction in game design circles suggests that you can more successfully assess potential engagement by focusing on the things that motivate engagement. The Player Experience of Need Satisfaction (PENS) model, developed by Scott Rigby and Richard Ryan of the consulting firm Immersyve and based on self-determination theory, proposes that three primary motivators drive players' subjective experience of a game:[3]

- **Competence**—the feeling that you are effective at what you're doing

- **Autonomy**—the feeling of freedom to make your own decisions and act on them

- **Relatedness**—the feeling of authentic connections to other people

You can measure for these motivators in a playtest session by having players complete short questionnaires immediately following important events in the game, such as a difficult puzzle or a pitched battle. For example, you might ask players to rate the extent to which they agree or disagree with these statements:

- "The game kept me on my toes but did not overwhelm me." (to measure competence)

- "I felt controlled and pressured to act a certain way." (to measure autonomy)

- "I formed meaningful connections with other people." (to measure relatedness)

Asking similar questions periodically over the course of gameplay, you can develop a map of the experiences in the game that most strongly support each of these drivers. Using these measures, Rigby and Ryan report that you can project outcomes such as the likelihood that players will purchase other games from the same developer or that they will recommend the game to others.[4]

Rigby and Ryan have demonstrated correlations among the three measures of motivation and player outcomes for specific genres of games. For example, the PENS measures were found to be very accurate at predicting the likelihood that players of an adventure or role-playing game would purchase more games from the same developer. However, PENS does not predict that same outcome as reliably for first-person shooter games. Figure 8.3 shows the strengths of the relationships that Rigby and Ryan have found in each of four genres.

---

3 Rigby, S., & Ryan, R. (2011). *Glued to games: How video games draw us in and hold us spellbound.* Santa Barbara, CA: Praeger, p. 10.

4 Ryan, R. M., Rigby, C. S., & Przybylski, A. (2006). The motivational pull of video games: A self-determination theory approach. *Motivation and Emotion, 30,* 344–360.

Relationship between PENS measures and important outcomes

Measures by genre	Player outcomes		
	Fun / enjoyment	Will buy more of developer's game	Will recommend game to others
Massively multiplayer online games			
Composite PENS	●●●	●●	●●●
Competence	●●	●●	●●
Autonomy	●●●	●●●	●●●
Relatedness	●●	●	●
First-person shooters			
Composite PENS	●●●	●●	●●
Competence	●●●	●●	●●
Autonomy	●●	●	●●
Relatedness	●	●	○
Adventure / role-playing games			
Composite PENS	●●●	●●●	●●●
Competence	●●	●●●	●●
Autonomy	●●●	●●●	●●●
Strategy games			
Composite PENS	●●●	●●	●●
Competence	●●	●●	●●
Autonomy	●●●	●●●	●●●

●●● Very strong relationship   ●● Strong relationship   ● Significant relationship   ○ No relationship

DATA FROM SCOTT RIGBY, IMMERSYVE

FIGURE 8.3

PENS measures were found to accurately predict specific player outcomes. The strength of the relationship varied by the genre of the game being played.

PENS is still maturing as an assessment method. More research is needed to discover how the importance of the three motivators changes for different types of players. There is not yet a robust accounting of outcomes that PENS can be used to project in other genres. And the findings across genres don't account for design variability within those genres (not all role-playing games play the same way). Still, the demonstrated success of PENS in predicting player outcomes speaks well of motivational models of engagement. With continued development, PENS or a similar method holds the promise of reducing the risk of design by predicting long-range outcomes from short-range measures.

An Easy Transition

Playtesting may be the part of game design where UX design generalists feel most at home. Although games require significant changes in the way we usually test, we're also accustomed to adapting our methods to accommodate a broad range of different interfaces, platforms, and design questions. It's not an enormous leap to adapt them to playtesting. Our skills in recruitment, test design, facilitation, debriefing, and synthesizing observations into actionable recommendations all translate directly.

Playtesting is in fact currently underpracticed by game design companies. As a UX designer, you may find that providing testing consulting services can serve as a good introduction to the game design discipline. It's a great opportunity to bring a valuable skill set to games while developing a critical eye for design.

Behavioral Tools

Every UX designer must also be, to some extent, a good psychologist. Understanding how people perceive and think about the world allows us to design user interfaces that make intuitive sense. Such expertise is important in game design as well. *Tetris* is very perceptual (as you try to figure out which piece is which) and very cognitive (as you decide where the pieces should be stacked). But there's also something else going on. Through its design, *Tetris* pulls you in and encourages you to keep going. Although you might have planned to play just one round when you first sat down, by the time it's over you feel like playing another, and then you end up playing a few more times, followed immediately by a few more rounds. The act of playing the game creates new drives that you didn't have when you first sat down to play.

In UX design, we're accustomed to supporting the drives that people bring to the experience, not determining what those drives should be. But video game designers have access to a powerful set of behavioral tools that can create new motivations for players, opening up a new angle on design that we usually don't have access to when working in user experience. These tools can be applied to engage people deeply in the game and involve them in constructing the experience. The principles underlying these tools were formally defined by the behaviorists—psychologists who based their study of the mind on the externally observable actions of human beings and animals.

It's very important to remember that these tools cannot generate interest in an uninteresting game, trick people into doing something they don't want to do, or hold people captive to an experience they don't enjoy. That's not the point. Instead, they create advantages for design by increasing the likelihood that players will adopt particular modes of play. Applied well, these tools can give shape to the gameplay and introduce more meaningful choices to the experience.

Because games give us access to this mode of design that's so far outside of the way we normally work, it's worth taking a moment to review the basics of behaviorism. After a primer, I'll present a pair of case studies examining how these elements of psychology underlie the success of two popular video games.

A Quick Guide to Behaviorism

A rat is placed inside a small box in a laboratory. On one side of the box is a lever and a chute (Figure 9.1). When the rat accidentally brushes against the lever, a food pellet comes flying down the chute. The rat gobbles it up, finding it very tasty. Then, while trying to find a way out through the top of the box, it props a front paw against the lever and another delicious pellet appears. Ooh, pellet! A few more such happy accidents, and the rat starts to catch on. Before long, it's pressing the lever repeatedly every time it feels hungry.

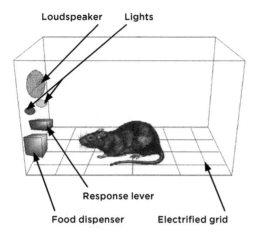

Loudspeaker   Lights

Response lever

Food dispenser   Electrified grid

FIGURE 9.1
Experiments using
animals in Skinner
boxes revealed
the effects that
environmental factors
can have on behavior.

Variations on this experiment, devised by behaviorist B. F. Skinner, demonstrated the basic principles of a form of learning called operant conditioning. In this type of learning, an animal or a person acts on the outside world, and the way the world responds makes it more or less likely that the behavior will be repeated in the future. Skinner showed that by manipulating the rules that control how the box's mechanism issues rewards and punishments, he could drive animals toward selected behaviors.

Notice that all of the characteristics of games described in Chapter 2 apply to the Skinner box as well:

- **An objective.** The animal is always working toward obtaining the food pellet.

- **Environmental constraints.** The animal is confined to a box and doesn't have access to food except through the feeding mechanism.

- **Formal constraints.** The animal must take a particular action, such as pressing a lever, to get the reward. It also must not perform other forbidden actions, such as pressing the wrong lever.

- **Machine-based arbitration.** The box's automated mechanism handles compliance with the rules and issues the rewards and punishments.

Skinner boxes, then, fall into the same class of devices as video games, pinball, pachinko, and slot machines. This commonality matters to us as designers because the same methods that allowed Skinner to shape the behavior of animals can also be applied to affect people's actions in games.

Consequences of Behavior

Reinforcement

When you give a reward for doing something, you make it more likely that action will be repeated. Giving a reward is called *reinforcing* the behavior, and there are two primary ways to do it.

When the rat gets a pellet for pressing the lever, it is receiving *positive reinforcement*. In other words, in response to performing a desired action, it receives something that it appreciates. People have their pellets too. One of my coworkers brings a bowl of candy with her every time she calls an especially tedious meeting. People come knowing they'll be bored to tears, but they also know they can at least look forward to some candy (these meetings do always happen to be well attended). Another example of positive reinforcement is leaving a big tip for a waiter who provides especially good service. Because tipping is a social norm, waiters know that, in general, the amount of money they make depends on the quality of the job they do.

The other way to reinforce a behavior is to alleviate people of something they don't like. This method is called *negative reinforcement*. People don't like to spend their hard-earned money. Because we have to pay money for almost everything, anything that's available for free or at a substantial discount is extremely attractive. Coffee shops, for example, capitalize on behaviorism by giving customers loyalty cards that award them a free cup of coffee after they buy 10. Governments encourage citizens to buy homes, save for retirement, and install solar panels by offering tax breaks. These incentives may not work for everyone, but they don't have to. By reducing their fees, coffee shops and governments increase the probability that people will do the things they want them to do.

Games are very good at offering players many different types of rewards, from points to unlockables to achievements. Chapter 10 examines these reward systems in depth.

Punishment

Sometimes the Skinner box is wired to dole out electric shocks when the poor rat does something the experimenter doesn't want it to do, such as pressing the lever when a red light is on. Punishment is reinforcement's sinister twin; it makes it less likely that an action will be repeated.

As with reinforcement, punishment can be applied in either of two ways. Getting zapped by a Skinner box is a form of *positive punishment*—having something negative inflicted as a disincentive to further action. Human beings tend to develop plenty of ways to punish, from small to big. Some parents spank their children; schools issue detentions, suspensions, and expulsions; police give out tickets for speeding and reckless driving; nations levy sanctions and impose trade tariffs on one another. *Negative punishment*, by contrast, takes away something valued or enjoyed, such as when parents ground their children or revoke driving privileges for acting irresponsibly.

Most UX design books don't spend much time discussing the merits of punishment as a design choice. But in game experiences, punishment is a tool at your disposal like any other, with appropriate and inappropriate uses. If a virtual-pet game is intended to teach players how to be responsible for the care of another living thing, then it's appropriate to set them back when they fail to live up to their responsibilities. Their pet may lose health points and then require more care from the player to bring it back to its previous level of health. Selective punishments can make a game experience more enjoyable because consequences are an inherent part of gameplay.

Considerations in the Design of Consequences

There are some important nuances in the ways that rewards and punishments work. Understanding these concepts is important, in part because it allows you to design more successful systems of consequences, and in part because it can shine a light on an opportunity to achieve something that you might have otherwise missed.

Timing

Reinforcements and punishments are more effective when they're given in a timely fashion so that there's a clear relationship between the action and its consequence. If a rat gets its pellet a full minute after pressing the lever, it's more likely to associate the reward with whatever it has moved on to doing at that point—taking a drink of water or cleaning its tail, for example. This type of confusion sometimes shows up in usability testing of conventional interfaces, as when a user is working with an unresponsive system and attributes changes on-screen to the wrong actions. Punishments that are administered too late will seem random, cruel, and beyond one's control. This is why, as discussed in Chapter 5, maintaining a clear relationship between actions and consequences is an important principle in game design as well.

Extinction

If a learned action suddenly stops producing the expected reward, you'll eventually give up. This response is called *extinction*. Very young children learn to cry more often when crying consistently gets them attention from grown-ups. Parents can break this behavior by withholding attention when it's clear that their child is just being a little dramatic. Role-playing games encourage players to continually invest in new weapons and magic spells by presenting them with new enemies that are less affected by the trusty old standbys. People stop using a website's search engine when it starts bringing back lousy results.

Defiance

One of the problems with punishment is that it discourages bad behavior only as long as the authority giving out the punishment is watching. In real life, people sometimes delight in being defiant when they feel they won't get caught. Fourth-graders wait until the teacher's back is turned to start passing notes and pulling hair. A teacher who leaves the classroom unsupervised altogether for 10 minutes can expect to return to mayhem. In the United States, Amazon.com doesn't collect the state sales taxes owed on purchases, and people generally neglect to pay them on their own, knowing that there is no one to enforce the rules.[1]

Some games actually turn defiance into an element of the gameplay. In *Grand Theft Auto*, a crime is punishable only if a police officer is nearby to observe it (Figure 9.2). If the crime goes unseen, the player can get away with it. Creative UX designers might use a similar strategy to explore questions of morality and ethics, challenging people to consider what they would be willing to do in situations where they believe no one would be willing to stop them, and then exposing them to the consequences of those actions.

ROCKSTAR GAMES

FIGURE 9.2
In *Grand Theft Auto IV*, crimes are punishable only when the police are around to see them.

---

1 Kopytoff, V. G. (2011, March 13). Amazon pressured on sales tax. *New York Times*.

Punishments can go too far. A single, especially sharp physical or psychological assault can be enough to discourage a person from ever trying the associated action again, and it could even result in a deep-seated fear of the person or thing that inflicted the trauma. One of the advantages of video games is that the player is always fundamentally safe. Although games can induce real fear, revulsion, or dread, there is never any true risk to the player's health or life. This shield from real consequences can create opportunities for people to explore dangerous or stressful situations in calm and rational ways through games. UX designers can make use of game design, for example, to help prepare emergency workers to handle disastrous events.

Schedules of Reinforcement

Behaviorists found that changing the frequency and timing of rewards and punishments creates specific, predictable patterns of behavior. Skinner defined several such schedules of reinforcement, each with its own distinct effects and its own implications for design.

Continuous Reinforcement

Continuous reinforcement is the simplest kind of schedule, with each desired action resulting in a reward (technically it isn't a schedule at all, but that's academic). New behaviors are picked up fastest with continuous reinforcement, so it's useful early in a game or within training levels. But because behaviors learned on a continuous schedule extinguish quickly if the reward suddenly stops coming, some things need to work reliably so that people can consistently count on them.

Continuous reinforcement is extremely important in the design of conventional user interfaces; in fact, it's normally the only way we UX designers work. If users find that menu items don't respond in a timely fashion when they're clicked, they'll stop trying pretty quickly. Game design, however, allows us to make use of other types of reinforcement schedules, each of which promotes different patterns of behavior.

Fixed-Ratio Schedules

A fixed-ratio schedule gives out the reward only after a predetermined number of tries. For example, a Skinner box might be set up to give the rat a pellet every fifth time it presses the lever. Rats respond to this schedule by working faster—pushing the lever very quickly until the pellet pops out, stopping to take a quick breather, and then going right back to tapping away at the lever (Figure 9.3). The same pattern happens in shooter games when enemies require a specific number of hits to be killed.

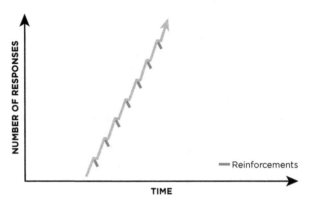

FIGURE 9.3
This is the behavior pattern produced when you have to do something a specific number of times to realize a payoff.

Variable-Ratio Schedules

On the variable-ratio schedule, the reward is given after a number of tries that changes over time (although there isn't a huge deviation from the average). The result is the fastest rate of response, with very little pausing after the reinforcement is given (Figure 9.4). Slot machines work on variable-ratio schedules. They pay out fairly regularly, but not predictably. You know a win is coming, but you don't know how many times you'll need to drop in a coin before it happens. This schedule of reinforcement is the reason players get hooked.

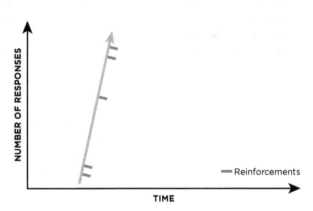

FIGURE 9.4
Here you get nothing unless you keep trying, and there's no way to know how many times you need to try.

Fixed-Interval Schedules

Rats in a box on a fixed-interval schedule receive a pellet only after a fixed amount of time. No matter how many times the lever is pressed, nothing will happen until the required time has elapsed. Once rats grow accustomed to this schedule, they lay off the lever for a while after getting a reward, and then start pressing it furiously right around the time they expect another pellet to become available (Figure 9.5).

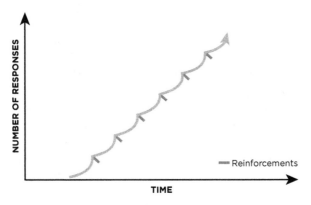

FIGURE 9.5
When the time interval is fixed, you gradually develop a feel for when you need to try, so you step up your efforts around the time you think they're going to pay off, and then you chill out for a bit.

Variable-Interval Schedules

In a variable-interval schedule, a reward is issued after an amount of time that keeps changing. From the rat's perspective, this sort of schedule is indistinguishable from randomization. This schedule produces the slowest pattern of behavior (Figure 9.6). Because the rat doesn't know exactly when the reward will come and tapping the lever faster doesn't help anything, it makes the most sense to check in only every now and then.

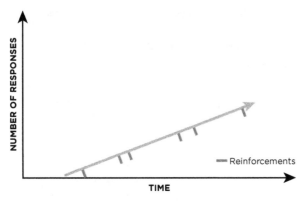

FIGURE 9.6
If the reward shows up only every now and then, with no regularity, you tend to relax because it's just not worth checking all the time.

Behaviorism in Video Games

You can use the principles of behaviorism to create a better game design. They enable you to create predictable patterns of behavior and craft an experience that will be more challenging, more interesting, and more engaging. I'll wrap up this chapter with a couple of examples that demonstrate the effects that these behavioral tools, applied carefully, have had in real-world games.

Pac-Man

When we look closely at games that a lot of people have played compulsively, we often find that these games contain examples of behaviorism in action. *Pac-Man*, for example, made use of several principles first observed in Skinner boxes.

Like many other arcade games, *Pac-Man*'s system of positive reinforcement is based on points. The points are just used as a common currency, providing a single way to reward several different types of actions commensurate with their difficulty. The small dots scattered over the board provide only 10 points each, but there are a lot of them. So clearing the board is a worthwhile long-term goal. Eating one ghost provides 200 points, with the reward doubling for each additional ghost eaten within a short period. But trying to eat multiple ghosts is risky, because their vulnerability may run out before the player gets to them. Forcing players to make a trade-off between earning points and staying safe makes the game more interesting and exciting.

Pac-Man also provides negative reinforcement. The game is continually stressful because the player is constantly being hunted by the ghosts and running to avoid being cornered, eaten, and short-changed on a perfectly good quarter. Eating a power pellet, however, temporarily alleviates the negative situation and allows the player to enjoy complete safety on the board. So the power pellets are very attractive, but only four of them are available. Consuming all of them too quickly leaves the player defenseless while still needing to clear the board. This design presents players with another meaningful choice: enjoy safety in the short term or maximize their chances of surviving in the long term.

Finally, the bonus fruits follow a fixed-interval schedule, appearing on the board at predetermined times (Figure 9.7). Players can gain the most points in the game by eating fruit, but again this strategy involves increased risk because the fruit appears in one of the most dangerous spots on the board and may disappear before the player can get to it. As players gain experience with the game, they become able to predict when the fruit will appear. As with all fixed-interval schedules, players can spend the time when they're not expecting the fruit engaged in other things, and then start hanging out around the lower middle of the board when they sense the fruit is about to pop up. The most experienced players are able to minimize risk by arriving at the drop point just as the fruit appears.

Left 4 Dead

Valve Software's online multiplayer game *Left 4 Dead* was designed expressly with principles of behaviorism in mind. It's set in a zombie apocalypse, with some players in the role of human survivors fighting other players in the role of the infected.

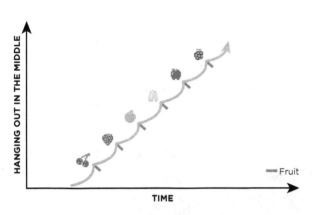

FIGURE 9.7
As with any fixed-interval schedule, the points offered by the opportunity to gobble up a piece of fruit in *Pac-Man* encourage players to start hanging out around the middle of the board when they think the next piece of fruit is about to appear.

One element of the design provides a great example of positive punishment being used to improve the gameplay experience. The game's designers wanted to create a teamwork dynamic in which players representing the humans would stick together as a group and help one another (Figure 9.8). To promote this form of play, they designed the abilities of the infected specifically so that human players who wandered away from the group would be easy pickings. The players' movements aren't directly restricted in any way, but players who decide to go rogue find themselves attacked and killed more often. The winning strategy comes from sticking with the group, working collaboratively, and building relationships with your team members.

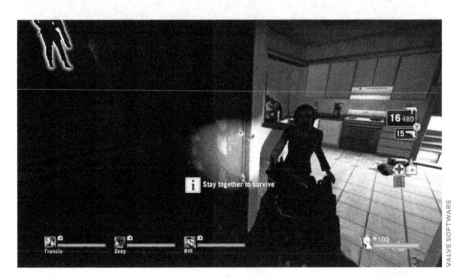

FIGURE 9.8
The designers of *Left 4 Dead* wanted to create a dynamic that encouraged players to stay together.

The item drops in *Left 4 Dead* make use of the behavior pattern that results from a variable-interval schedule of reinforcement. Every so often, a helpful item, like a weapon or health pack, will appear at fixed locations in the game world (Figure 9.9). All experienced players know where the items will show up, but they don't know when. As a result, they need to keep checking these spots regularly or someone else will pick them up first. So it is more likely that players will be found at certain locations on the map at any given time—knowledge that their opponents can use to their own advantage by lying in ambush nearby.

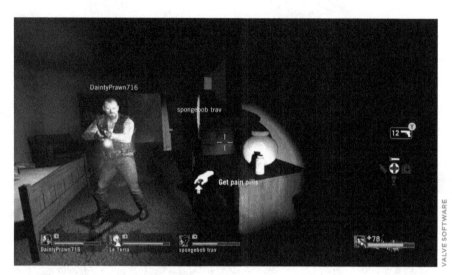

FIGURE 9.9
Item drops use reinforcement schedules to increase the likelihood that players will revisit specific places frequently.

Note here that the game's designers aren't the only ones involved in creating the game experience. The players need to behave in a certain way for the gameplay to really work. The designers manipulate the system of play, and in reacting to that system the players construct the experience. This design promotes a deep level of engagement in the game.

What about Free Will?

Behaviorism can offend our sense of human dignity because it suggests that unseen actors can make our choices for us. Indeed, Skinner championed the ideas that our actions are determined by external forces rather than our own free will, and that our sense of self-determination is an illusion. Contemporary psychology has demonstrated that in real life, decision making is much more complex. People's internal capacity to think and reason can resist efforts to shape their behavior from the outside. But behaviorism did reveal a framework underlying the actions of most animals, which can also bear an influence on us—especially when we're inclined to allow it to.

Unlike Skinner's rats, video game players are not tyrannically confined to a box. They enter a game freely because they value the experience of playing. When players adopt collaborative gameplay strategies in response to the behavioral design of *Left 4 Dead*, it's not because their free will has been stolen away from them. They collaborate because it's the winning strategy that the game's designers have selected, and the players feel invested in winning. Such investment speaks well of the game's fundamental appeal, because people wouldn't feel so invested if they didn't enjoy the experience in the first place. The decision to play is an expression of our free will. When we cross into a game's magic circle, we acquiesce to its behavioral drivers in order to enable the experience.

Importantly, designs that don't value the player experience cannot be made enjoyable simply by applying the behavioral tools discussed in this chapter. If this were true, then creating compelling game experiences would be as easy as it is in the online parody *Progress Wars* (Figure 9.10). However, designers can make great use of these tools to deepen engagement in a game that is fundamentally rewarding to play.

FIGURE 9.10
Take *Mafia Wars*, remove all challenge, narrative, and meaning, and you're left with *Progress Wars*.

CHAPTER 10

Rewards in Games

W hatever people expect from a game experience, rewards always sweeten the deal. Think of rewards as gifts given to players in recognition of their efforts. Players are your guests, doing you the courtesy of spending time interacting with your creation. Offering something in return can show appreciation for their time while acknowledging their success and acumen. Rewards are worthwhile for two important reasons: they create meaningful measures of the player's performance, and they help sustain interest in the experience over time.

Even better, rewards in games can be incredibly cheap to make. This is one of the breathtaking efficiencies unique to virtual environments. In the physical world, producing anything carries costs for design, materials, labor, transportation, fuel, storage, and so on. And each item produced can be sold only one time, so a sufficient quantity must be sold to justify their cost.

But in a virtual world, production costs virtually nothing once a reliable system of rewards is set up. Instead of working with real materials, you construct objects out of raw information. A virtual house in *FarmVille* is nothing more than a few fields in a database and a handful of image assets. Once you have those elements, you can sell the house an infinite number of times. People ascribe real value to it because of its significance to the gameplay.

The value of intangible things is not completely alien to conventional UX design. Users will pay real money for digital greeting cards, desktop wallpaper, and irritating ringtones. But virtual rewards can have much richer meaning in the context of a game world, where they can impart advantages to the player and serve as positive reinforcements for effective play.

Common Reward Systems

There are many well-established ways in which game designers reward players, as well as new and innovative systems that are emerging from the explosive growth of the video game industry. It's great to have such a variety of rewards, because they each have different effects on players and different advantages for design. Collectively, reward systems make up a tool kit that the designer can use to shape the gameplay experience. This section reviews some of the most frequently used rewards, and explains how you can best put them to use.

Praise

One of the most effective ways to reward players for their work is also among the most overlooked. Simple praise for success creates a sense of accomplishment and appeals to players motivated by the need for accomplishment, competence, or even social image (see Chapter 4). Giving players this kind of acknowledgment can promote the sense that they are effective, and that their efforts are worthwhile.

Brain Age, a game for the Nintendo DS handheld gaming system that puts players through a battery of tests of their mental agility, strongly emphasizes praise, which is offered by the disembodied head of a Japanese neurologist (Figure 10.1). As players complete different cognitive exercises, Dr. Ryuta Kawashima comments on how well they're doing. When players show substantial improvement, his jaw drops and his eyes bulge as he breathlessly showers them with his congratulations. He is designed to provide the payoff that performance-oriented people desire.

FIGURE 10.1
The ever-supportive
Dr. Kawashima is an
important part of the
player experience of
Brain Age.

NINTENDO

Frequent praise tied to low-level success conditions can form a kind of positive background tone to a game. Using different tiers of emphasis can also nudge players toward better performance. This approach is common in dancing and music games, which often rate each dance step or guitar strum as "OK," "Great," or "Perfect!" Games like *Guitar Hero* and *Rock Band* push this positive feedback even further into fantasy with cheering audiences. One of the cleverest features of Nike+ (discussed in more detail in Chapter 11) allows people's friends to cheer them on while they're running.

Praise is cheap to implement and easy to apply consistently, and it can be very effective. It's a great way to start endearing your game to players and shouldn't be neglected for more complex types of rewards. But praise can accomplish only so much, as it has limited power to compel players to continue the experience for extended periods. It's also important not to overdo praise, which, if overly fawning, can easily ring insincere.

Point Systems

Points provide a uniform way of ranking separate instances of play relative to one another. They are simultaneously a measure of:

- **Performance**—how well the player has done in this particular sitting

- **Proficiency**—the level of skill obtained through practice

- **Progress**—how far the player has advanced in the game

Point systems appeal strongly to the need for competence because they quantify the overall quality of play and provide an absolute way of knowing whether you're doing better or worse compared to prior sittings or to other players.

Of course, point systems are not at all uncommon in UX design, where they are used most often as measures of reputation or quality (Figure 10.2). On Ebay, points are used to indicate the reliability of sellers, which can influence a buyer's decision to place a bid. Amazon and Netflix collect customer ratings and aggregate them into stars and histograms to help people compare different products. Amazon even layers a rating system on top of its rating system by letting users vote for whether a review was helpful or unhelpful. Digg allows users to elevate the visibility of news stories by giving them a thumbs-up or thumbs-down. Connections on LinkedIn serve as an implicit proxy for a person's professional standing. Likes on Facebook indicate preferences for just about anything.

FIGURE 10.2
Variations in point systems used around the Web.

I want to be careful not to imply that points can or should simply be tacked onto any experience. Points have no value in and of themselves. Rather, they are valuable for the contextual, emotional, and communal effects they can achieve. Both UX design and game design have innovated ways to put point systems to constructive use, creating a great opportunity for each to learn from the practices developed by the other. A few lessons from game design follow.

Many Actions, One Measure

A key advantage of point systems is that they allow many unrelated types of low-level success to be rolled up into a single, comprehensive number.

A platforming game may award points for perfectly executing a jump, successfully dispatching an enemy, picking up coins, finding a secret door, and finishing a level. Though each of these accomplishments speaks to a different skill or element of play, they all translate into the same common reward. In this way, points can simplify play.

Point systems should be applied only in places where they add specific value. If a role-playing game awards points for winning battles but what really matters to the game's advancement is the level of the player's character, then there's not much point in points. If it is a redundant reward, a point system can make the gameplay more complex than it needs to be.

Variation and Balance

Appropriately varying the number of points given for different actions can give a game greater depth. For example, giving substantially more points for riskier actions can provide an incentive for players to break away from safer habits and test their level of skill. Having a very broad range of points tied to many different types of actions can also support more strategic play, allowing players to pursue high scores in different ways.

Be careful, however, that you don't inadvertently create ways for players to exploit the point system. Awarding too many points for something can prompt players to pursue that one action to the exception of anything else, making the other elements of the game superfluous. When Harry Potter captures the snitch in Quidditch, so many points are awarded that the other players might as well not have bothered to show up. A game's point system needs to be carefully *balanced* through prototyping and playtesting.

Leaderboards

You scored 1,529,837 points—WHOOPEE! But wait, how do you know whether that's good or bad? Points don't really mean anything if players don't have some way of comparing them to other instances of play. Leaderboards give points meaning by putting scores in context. They also extend interest in the game by giving players an objective to work toward.

At one level, leaderboards can support players who are trying to improve their game by allowing them to see their personal performance over separate instances of play. *Brain Age* actually charts players' progress over time, helping them to visualize how fast they're improving (or getting worse). Self-tracking extends interest in the game by giving players benchmarks to work toward.

More broadly, leaderboards let players see where they stand relative to other people playing the game. A common mistake in the design of leaderboards is to show only the top 10 or so players. Although restricting the list in this way rightly serves the interests of the people in those 10 slots, it doesn't let novice players know where they rank in the overall list. Avoid this problem by always automatically showing a logged-in player's rankings on the leaderboard. You could also divide the list more finely by showing the top performers over different periods (today, this week, this month) or by tracking different attributes (speed, completeness, popularity).

Online leaderboards are wonderfully easy to do in a networked world. They also make compelling social rewards possible by showing players where they stand relative to their specific circle of friends. All the better if you can offer players some means of bragging about their performance.

Currencies

Like points, currencies can be awarded in exchange for small wins throughout the session of play. They also similarly appeal to the players' need to feel competent by recognizing their skill. But currencies differ from points in that they both grow over time and can also be spent in various ways to benefit the player in the game. So currencies are an embedded element of the gameplay itself.

General and Specialized Currencies

It's useful to group currencies by two major types. *General currencies* work just like money in the real world; they can be spent on anything. They may give the player access to new kinds of weapons, properties, clothing, decorations, and so on. In multiplayer experiences, people can exchange money with one another for services or as bribes. The monetary systems of some modern online multiplayer games have grown into robust economies in their own right. In *EVE Online*, for example, goods in the game are priced by supply and demand.

In contrast, *specialized currencies* may be spent only on specific things. Specialized currencies are very common in role-playing games, which allow players to build characters around preferred attributes. Players may earn experience points or even more specialized currencies, such as intelligence points or cooking skill points. Players can then choose to spend these points on attributes like speed, strength, dexterity, magic power, or Thai cuisine. In this way, players can adapt the gameplay experience to suit the way they prefer to play. This approach appeals to players whose motivations lean toward autonomy.

Scarcity

Game currencies create a more engaging experience by forcing players to make decisions about how their earnings can best be applied. So the scarcity of the currency is important; its availability must be balanced against the cost of the things on which it can be spent. The player is then forced to make trade-offs among the available options. As discussed in Chapter 3, a great way to make games more interesting is to ask the player to make meaningful choices.

Scarcity also compels players to do the things the game asks them to do. If it were too easy to make money, the currency system would lose its challenge and the work of the game would become pointless. Suppose a role-playing game contained dungeons full of enemies, each of which paid anywhere between 1 and 20 gold pieces when it was defeated; but right outside of the dungeon there was a magic fountain that paid players 60 gold pieces a minute simply for standing next to it. Why would anyone then choose to go through the dungeon? Striking it rich may have its perks, but it undercuts the appeal of good hard work.

Games often present players with simple, highly visible meters that keep people aware of the scarcity of vital currencies. Forgive a quick digression: I've often thought that my life would benefit from having similar visualizations of the scarcity of time or money. It couldn't be that complicated for Microsoft Outlook to calculate the amount of time I have outside of scheduled meetings before the end of the day and present it as something akin to a health bar, right there on my desktop (Figure 10.3).

FIGURE 10.3
Seriously, can I
have this?

Other Important Differences from Point Systems

If you're trying to decide whether your game should have a point system or a currency system, there are two other factors you should weigh. First, currencies pose a much larger design challenge than do simple points. With currency systems, you need to plan for additional overhead to brainstorm items that can be purchased, assign attributes to them, design image assets for them, balance them, test them, and price them appropriately.

Second, currencies are generally better suited to games played over an extended period and in situations that allow players to save their work. The ability to pick up where you left off and build off of prior success certainly enhances the value of the currency. Point systems work perfectly well with game experiences that can be completed in a single sitting.

Leveling

Many games organize the development of a player's character into levels. These are stepped plateaus that the player ascends over the course of the game by completing required tasks. The player typically earns some form of points each time a task is completed, and the character is promoted to the next level when enough points have been accumulated. At each advance to the next level, the character's attributes are enhanced in some way. Think of the programs run by financial institutions that give lower fees and greater privileges to customers who hold progressively higher minimum balances. (Think, too, about how such programs might benefit from the design practices pioneered by game designers, to be described shortly.)

Leveling gives the player a sense of growing personal power. Over time, the character will journey from a nearly powerless role to a dominant one. Things that were once very difficult to do will become much easier, and the player will be ready to surmount new kinds of challenges. Leveling appeals to motivations of catharsis, accomplishment, and competence.

Structuring Gameplay

Leveling can benefit a game's design by giving structure to the gameplay and by providing players with a basis for understanding their progress through that structure. Designers can take advantage of these benefits by relating events in the game to the character's level.

Games' leveling systems typically contain some challenges that simply aren't attainable by players at lower levels. There are two common ways of making certain challenges available to only some players. First, designers can hard-code a minimum required level to perform an action. For example, a fantasy-adventure game might allow only a level-20 mage or higher to wield a golden scepter, which is itself necessary to gain access to the castle tower. Alternatively, progress may just be prohibitively difficult for characters with lesser attributes, as when a castle is guarded by a troll whose attributes are so strong that it makes swift work of any player below level 17. Either approach is helpful for design because it can create structure across the entire game environment, allowing the chapters of the game to unfold progressively.

Levels as a Reinforcement Schedule

Leveling systems represent a variation on schedules of reinforcement beyond those defined by Skinner (see Chapter 9). Players are on a fixed schedule, in that the point at which they reach the next level is predetermined and knowable. But the schedule isn't fixed either by ratio or by interval. Instead, players are aware of the number of experience points they need to reach the next level. The result is a behavior pattern similar to that of a fixed-interval schedule, in which players work harder when they know they're close to reaching the next level.[1]

Designers can enhance the "stickiness" of a leveling system in two ways. First, players need to feel that the next level is attainable. If the levels are too widely spaced, then players will start to give up (extinction). Successful

---

1 Von Ahn, L., & Dabbish, L. (2008, August). General techniques for designing games with a purpose. *Communications of the ACM, 51*(8), 63.

games typically contain dozens of levels, and dedicated players can often get through at least one in a single sitting. Second, players must feel that the effort is worthwhile. Upon reaching a new level, the enhancement made to a player's character should be significant enough that the difference is noticeable. The enhancement can be slight, but the player should have some sense that things have improved.

Extending Interest

Levels can help extend interest in the game far beyond the amount of time players would have otherwise spent playing. Many games require players to repeat similar actions over and over to gain enough experience points to reach the next level. This is a sneaky way of artificially turning less game into a longer gameplay experience. Without the clear objective provided by the leveling system, players would have no reason to fight the same orcs or gelatinous cubes over and over again. Of course, there's a limit to a player's tolerance for repetition. But well-designed levels can lighten the burden on design and development by getting more use out of the game's assets.

Customization

The ability to acquire and customize virtual possessions has become a common feature in modern video games. Clearly, the ability to customize virtual possessions appeals strongly to the need for creativity. But it also promotes a sense of investment within the game world, giving players something uniquely their own. In addition, customization offers social rewards by allowing players to showcase their work, enabling self-expression.

Levels of Customization

A customization dynamic can be incorporated at many different levels of the game's design:

- **The physical appearance of the player's avatar.** Miis, for example, are part of the unique charm of the Nintendo Wii's user interface (Figure 10.4).

FIGURE 10.4
Miis are an integral part of the Wii experience, literally putting the player right inside the game.

- **The avatar's clothing, jewelry, and hairstyle** (Figure 10.5). Similarly, many racing games allow players to customize their cars with paint, decals, rims, and other bling.

FIGURE 10.5
In *Grand Theft Auto IV*, players customize the appearance of their avatar by changing the clothes he wears.

- **Construction of the avatar's home.** *The Sims* provides a very open building interface that allows players to decide where each wall should be to create a home's living spaces (Figure 10.6).

FIGURE 10.6
The intuitive drag-and-build interface for putting an addition on the house in *The Sims*.

- **Decoration of the avatar's home.** *Animal Crossing* provides players with a vast number of home decorations, from area rugs to jukeboxes to video game systems (Figure 10.7). Functional decorations that play music or cook food add further appeal to customization.

NINTENDO

FIGURE 10.7
An elaborately decorated house in *Animal Crossing*, complete with indoor plants, slot machine, nesting dolls, and giant totems.

- **The game itself.** Some games provide players with a level editor. *LittleBigPlanet* lets players create and share their own fully fledged video games using a simple but comprehensive set of editor controls (Figure 10.8).

SONY COMPUTER ENTERTAINMENT

FIGURE 10.8
LittleBigPlanet provides an in-game editor, allowing players to construct their own games.

Customization serves as a reward when it's tied to a monetary system in the game. As players earn more money, they can afford increasingly expensive goods. Offering items in a broad range of price points encourages players to set objectives, dedicate themselves to the work of the game, and smoothly ascend a continuous grade to greater and greater prosperity. This steady, gradual climb contrasts with the stepped structure of a leveling system (Figure 10.9), and it gives the player greater control over the experience.

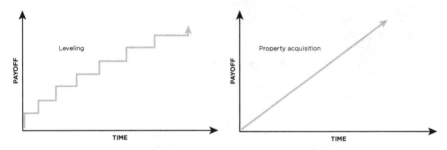

FIGURE 10.9
Whereas a leveling system provides a periodic payoff (left), items that players can purchase to customize their experience allow access to a steady flow of rewards (right).

Social Rewards

Customization options offer a much bigger payoff when players have the opportunity to share their creations online with one another. *FarmVille* encourages players to invite their friends to play the game, and then situates their farms adjacent to each other. Some players construct elaborate and sprawling estates, inspiring other players and giving them a reason to engage with the game (Figure 10.10).

FIGURE 10.10
An important part of the appeal of *FarmVille* is the opportunity to show off your fancy farm to your friends when they pop in for a visit.

Item Drops

One of the best-established video game patterns is a play area peppered with assorted health packs, weapons, and other items that give players new capabilities. Although such item drops may not be very realistic, they are an effective way to shape player behavior while adding interest to the gameplay experience.

Play Dynamics

Item drops can affect the way players experience the game in several ways:

- They may be used to lure players into taking greater risks. In a racing game, a particularly desirable power-up may be placed right on the edge of a cliff. Such a design creates a meaningful choice for players, forcing them to evaluate their own skill and weigh the benefits of success against the consequences of failure.

- They can provide hints or encourage players to discover new areas in the game. Being able to see an item is a cue to the player that there must be some way of getting to it even if that path isn't immediately apparent. The effort needed to reach the item can deepen the player's interest in the game.

- They can foster competition in multiplayer games by giving people something to fight over. In this way, the items reward players both for their skill and for their familiarity with the game.

- They can enable strategic play. The game may be balanced in such a way that players gain different advantages by chasing specific types of items. For example, some players in a multiplayer shooter may favor picking up invisibility power-ups, whereas others may seek out more powerful weapons to improve their offense or pick up armor for defense. In each case, the experience of the game might be very different.

Drop Locations and Schedules

Items may be programmed to appear again and again in the game environment. Where and when the drops occur further alter the gameplay. As shown in Figure 10.11, different types of locations and schedules may be combined to produce different effects in the game.

- Fixed locations with fixed schedules reward the players who are most familiar with the game. Experienced players will start hanging out at the known drop locations right around the scheduled drop time.

- Fixed locations with variable schedules reward persistence. The uncertainty about when an item will appear encourages players to revisit the same spot frequently.

- Variable locations with fixed schedules reward exploration. When players know that the right amount of time has passed, they will begin to check different likely places.

- Variable locations with variable schedules don't reward any particular behavior. This combination brings a stronger element of luck into the game, which favors both experienced and inexperienced players equally.

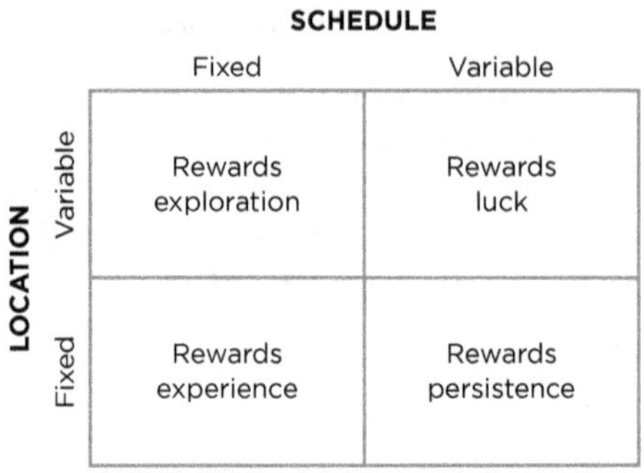

FIGURE 10.11
Different decisions about the timing and location of item drops have different results, making these considerations important factors of the reward system's design.

SCHEDULE

	Fixed	Variable
LOCATION Variable	Rewards exploration	Rewards luck
LOCATION Fixed	Rewards experience	Rewards persistence

Item Types

As the game designer, you can add another twist to the gameplay by varying the types of items that appear at the drop location, themselves on either a fixed or variable rotation.

Some items may provide players with a tangible benefit. A positive reinforcement will give the player something desirable, such as a speed boost in a racing game or a powerful weapon in a shooter. A negative reward will temporarily alleviate something undesirable from the gameplay. For example, the star in *Mario Kart* makes players temporarily impervious to attacks.

Dropped items might also punish players who carelessly pick them up. Punishments can be very effective in racing games, where players' momentum may carry them into an item even though they're trying to avoid it. Punishments may also be positive, as with a bomb that inflicts direct damage; or negative, as with a flat tire that robs players of speed.

Collections

Many popular games challenge players to collect items from a fixed available set, which are retained in the player's inventory rather than being spent or lost. Collectible items have a specialness that stands apart from the appeal of points, currencies, or item drops.

Collection systems take advantage of a natural human inclination to find, capture, and hold on to things. My first job out of graduate school was at the

Web agency iXL Enterprises, which had a unique recognition program that gave one of three awards, each representing a letter in the company's name. The "i" award was given for innovation; the "X" award was given for extra effort; and the "L" award was given for leadership. Each came with a trophy for the letter, and the three trophies snapped together to form the complete logo. Some people were highly motivated to collect all three, and in pursuing them they worked in ways that the company valued. Where some people are driven to collect interlocking trophies, others are drawn to stamps or coins. The desires for symmetry and completion can make collections powerful motivators.

Means of Collection

As a game designer, you can capitalize on people's inclination to collect by structuring challenges around the promise of acquiring more stuff. Broadly, there are three ways that collectible items may be acquired in a game:

- **Earned items** are awarded when the player accomplishes something in the game. This is an easy way to motivate players to take on a game's challenges. *Pokémon*, for example, requires players to win fights to fill out their collection of brightly colored monsters.

- **Found items** require the player to go on a kind of Easter egg hunt through the game environment to find the hidden items. This design encourages exploration, which works well in expansive game worlds. The *Grand Theft Auto* games, for example, contain multiple collection systems requiring players to steal certain cars, find hidden packages of drugs, and paint over gang graffiti. Players who take on these optional challenges discover the impressive size of the virtual environment.

- **Purchased items** combine a collection system with a currency system to create an even more compelling reward system. The advantage of using game money to acquire collectible items is that many different types of actions—fighting, working, trading—can be translated into ownership of the items.

Size and Difficulty

A collection system's capacity to hold players' interest in the game is a function of the size of the collection and of the difficulty of acquiring the collectible items.

An entire set of collectibles commonly comprises dozens or even hundreds of items. Because such large collections are very conventional, you shouldn't be too concerned about overdoing it. Besides, a large collection allows players to collect until their interest in it naturally expires, instead of being cut off early. However, if the size of the collection is so vast as to seem unattainable, then players may start to wonder whether they should even bother trying.

Most games that include collection systems provide a range of difficulties for acquiring items. It's beneficial to have a large number of items that can be acquired quite easily. Quickly finding a number of items gives players the sense that collecting is an attainable and worthwhile objective, while providing them a taste of the collection dynamic. Gradually increasing the difficulty to the point where a few items are very hard to obtain allows the collection dynamic to naturally keep pace with the player's growing skill and familiarity with the game environment.

Achievements

Achievements are one of the newer developments in game design and have exploded in popularity in recent years to become one of the most recognizable conventions in contemporary gaming. Achievements form a kind of metagame that rides on top of the formal game experience. They invite the player to dive very deeply into the gameplay and perform difficult or unusual things just for the sake of having done them. They take advantage of the drive that inspires some people to climb mountains, appealing strongly to the motivation of accomplishment.

Flexibility

A major design advantage of achievements is that they can be awarded for absolutely anything. You name it: Escaping the enemy compound without killing anyone. Causing a pileup involving at least 10 cars. Collecting every coin in a particular level. Anything that can actually happen in the game can make for a good achievement. This flexibility allows designers to reward players for taking a very active interest in the game, and pursuing achievements lets players gain an appreciation for the extent of the game design.

Cheap and Easy

Achievements involve very little design overhead. They ask the player to perform something that could be done in the game anyway *but might not otherwise be necessary*. They may, for example, ask the player to complete a level without using any health packs. Nothing in the game design prevents the player from attempting to do that, but without the achievement as a motivator, the player would have had no reason to try it.

So the game itself can remain exactly the way it is without any special accommodation to support achievements. The only development costs are in creating sniffer programs to detect when the player has met the requirements of each achievement, in alerting the player, and in designing an interface that displays the achievements.

Skill Level

Because achievements are so cheap and easy to create, many games offer dozens of them. That's great, because then designers can accommodate a broad range of player skill levels, from complete novice to seasoned master. As a result, more players can feel like beneficiaries of the reward system, which can make the game feel accessible.

Challenge is good for players who really want to be tested, but make sure you never ask the impossible. Always test your achievements to be certain that the thing the player is required to do can actually be done. Sending someone off to pursue something that's impossible is a special kind of cruelty.

Known versus Hidden Objectives

Achievement systems vary by whether or not they tell the player what's required of them. Each approach offers different advantages.

Known objectives keep players moving forward by always providing achievements that people can work toward. If you're concerned about drop-off in play, consider achievements with known objectives.

Hidden objectives don't tell players exactly what they need to do to get the achievement. Sometimes a clue might be provided, such as the name of the achievement without its description. Players need to make some guesses about which things will score them an achievement, which may or may not pay off. Hidden objectives reward self-motivated interest in the game.

Clearly it's important that achievements with hidden objectives be somewhat intuitive and be awarded for logical challenges in the game. But they can also pay off in their surprise. *Animal Crossing* awards an achievement for standing completely still for five minutes. At some point in time, most players will set the controller down while they attend to something else, only to be delighted to find their inactivity rewarded.

Unlockables

Sometimes you may want to reward players with something more substantive to recognize their accomplishments. One approach is to allow players to unlock special content that otherwise remains unavailable to them.

Common Forms

Just about anything you design in the game that isn't essential to the core gameplay can be turned into unlockable content, and the actions that players have to complete to unlock them can be as flexible as those for achievements.

Advanced gameplay modes are a common form of unlockable content. These are harder levels that are unlocked once the player completes the game on an easier setting. When players start a game in *Halo*, they can see that a mode called "Legendary" exists, described tauntingly in this way:

> You face opponents who have never known defeat, who laugh in alien tongues at your efforts to survive. This is suicide.

But players can't access the Legendary mode until they complete the normal difficulty level. This is a smart approach because it gives players access to the harder mode only when they're ready for it. This kind of unlockable content can significantly extend players' time in the game by appealing to their need to feel competent.

Other games allow players to unlock more parts of the story line as they progress through the game. Fighting games like *Tekken* often play a cinematic cutscene each time the player successfully completes the game with one of the characters, filling in that character's backstory. After they're unlocked, players can access the cutscenes again at any time through a cinema library. Narrative elements like these build the richness of the game world, prioritizing the player's need for immersion. But it also parcels out the narrative in small doses, asking something of the player first.

Maximizing the Benefit of Unlockables

Unlockables can substantially benefit the design by giving players something to work toward. The major disadvantage of unlockables is that they deliberately make a portion of the game unavailable to the player. So the effort that went into developing the special content will be wasted on those players who don't manage (or care) to unlock them. As the game designer, you should carefully weigh the cost of creating content against the probability that players will actually experience it.

You can maximize the cost-benefit ratio of locked content in a few ways:

- Make sure players are aware that the unlockable content is available. Whet their appetite with teasers or empty libraries from which the content will be accessed.

- Control the difficulty of the tasks players need to complete to unlock the content. If the tasks are too challenging, players might feel discouraged and decide not to try.

- Conduct playtesting to make sure that a sufficient proportion of players will actually feel motivated to try to unlock the content and will have the ability to do so.

Metarewards

Some rewards exist outside of the game world altogether and are instead about the experience of playing the game.

Easter Eggs

The first "Easter egg"—a secret hidden inside the interface—was a developer credit screen in the 1975 game *Adventure* for the Atari 2600. Easter eggs are a wink to the player from the people who made the game. They reward players for taking an active interest in the game and exploring its environment. People don't know that the Easter eggs are there, but rather stumble across them. Because there can be no active effort to locate Easter eggs, they can't be used to motivate players to take certain actions.

Easter eggs can, however, reward players by delighting them with an unexpected surprise, especially when players have just had to do something elaborate or challenging. There's an area in the middle of the virtual city in *Grand Theft Auto III* that is surrounded by high walls with no steps or ladders nearby. Players can reach the area only by parking cars of different heights along the wall, climbing up from one to the next, and then jumping to the other side. The player then turns around to see a message written on the wall: "You weren't supposed to be able to get here you know."

Cheats

Many game designers deliberately build in cheat codes, in which the player executes improbable button presses that change the conditions inside the game. Cheats may, for example, instantly give the player all the weapons in the game, restore all health, grant invincibility, or bestow other favorable shortcuts to regular play.

But is cheating okay? Wouldn't allowing cheating be ethically dubious? Wouldn't it undermine your game's carefully balanced design? Perhaps surprisingly, some game theorists urge designers to have sympathy for the cheater.[2] After all, people cheat because they want to improve their experience of the game. In a way, they're showing that they value the game's outcome; they're just dissatisfied with the conditions for success that the design places on them.

Building cheat codes into a game rewards players for taking an interest in it. Of course, doing so sacrifices the designer's intended experience. But when players are willing to cheat rather than deal with the obstacles you've created for them, this might be the better trade-off. Players might otherwise decide to bail on the game altogether, so cheats can give you a second chance to keep them inside the experience.

---

2   Salen, K., & Zimmerman, E. (2004). *Rules of play: Game design fundamentals.* Cambridge, MA: MIT Press, p. 275.

In addition, no one gets hurt if the player is only cheating the computer running the game. The circuits will take no offense and will hardly notice the injustice they've suffered. Still, there are two situations when cheating does become a real problem. In the first case, other real people are the victims of the cheater. If there's a multiplayer aspect to your game, allowing players to cheat destroys the experience for everyone else. In the second case, the game pays out some kind of reward in the real world, which is the subject of the next section.

External Rewards

Some games go a step further and offer players tangible rewards such as money, prizes, or special privileges. Such external rewards offer players something beyond the joys that are to be found within the game itself.

Risks

A clear disadvantage to this approach is that it requires someone to lay out additional money. However, designers can mitigate this drawback by paying out rewards that defray their own expense. Coupons, for example, can drive business by bringing new customers into stores.

External rewards also can't make up for the shortcomings of a lousy game. In the early 1990s, a video game called *Treasure Quest* lured players in with the promise of a $1 million prize to the first person to correctly solve all of its puzzles. The experience of playing through the game's bizarre and incomprehensible interface, however, was miserable. *Treasure Quest* has long since been forgotten, and the experiment has not been repeated.

But there's another, more subtle risk to offering players external rewards. Significant research since the 1960s has shown that in the real world, such rewards produce actions that are of lower quality: less creative, less thoughtful, and less accurate. The reason is that these external rewards have no effect on people's underlying motivations to take action in the first place; the reward is sought only for the sake of the reward. There is no improved regard for the activity itself.[3]

I must mention that this research also implicates praise, point systems, collections, and other rewards like those that I've already discussed. But I would argue that it doesn't apply to the game world, because the game world is an imaginary space that players willingly enter girded with unalloyed motivation to enjoy intangible success. These rewards must be understood as a part of the gameplay experience itself, since they have no tangible manifestation beyond its boundaries. Only when rewards regress

---

3 Kohn, A. (1993). *Punished by rewards*. Boston, MA: Houghton Mifflin, pp. 35–48.

outward from the game's magic circle into the real world do they become problematic, because the prospect of a real payoff can overshadow the intrinsic delights of engaging with the game. The gameplay can then come to be seen as drudgery standing in the way of the player's real goal. This effect is destructive to the experience, and a real problem for design.

Games Must Be Intrinsically Rewarding

The video game industry has proven to be fantastically successful without offering players anything tangible in return. That's because the act of playing a good game is itself inherently enjoyable. Intrinsic rewards have such demonstrated success that they are pervasive in game design. If all you offer as a reason to play is external rewards, then what you're left with is something closer to an incentives program.

Nonetheless, I would stop short of completely ruling out a role for external rewards in game design. Clearly, such rewards work for roulette, lotteries, and game shows. But for the reasons I've discussed, they can also cheapen the gameplay experience. Any decision to implement a system of external rewards should be taken with full awareness of this risk. If you do choose to offer an external reward—say, to spark interest in your game—you'll be most successful if you rely on more captivating intrinsic reasons to keep people playing.

Combining Game Rewards

When you're designing a game, one of the first things you should consider is how long you expect people to play it. Many short game experiences need only a single reward system. *Pong* has no game currency, no levels, no power-ups, no clothing options, no Easter eggs, no cheat codes—and it offers very little in the way of story line (line hits dot, dot flies into hole). Points alone are quite sufficient for *Pong*.

On the other hand, people don't play *Pong* all that long. Modern games can last weeks or months, and over that kind of time frame you need much more to keep things interesting. That's why many games today incorporate multiple reward systems into the experience. *Grand Theft Auto*, for example, uses nearly all of the reward systems described in this chapter. Players who grow bored with the story line can turn their focus to earning money, tracking down hidden items, customizing their characters' hair and clothing, or filling out their collections of achievements.

Games sometimes nest their reward systems so that players need to obtain one reward to gain access to another one. In *Final Fantasy*, the money that players earn from battles allows them to purchase better armor and weapons, which enable them to win more battles, which allows them to level up their characters, which unlocks the story line.

Size your reward systems appropriately for the ambition of your design. More rewards mean that more time and effort are required to plan, balance, and implement them, but well-executed rewards can pay you back immeasurably in the quality of the gameplay experience.

CHAPTER 11

Games for
Action

Conventional UX design can be intrinsically limiting in that it's centrally concerned with supporting the objectives that users already have when they arrive at the experience, whether that's balancing their checkbook, reconnecting with high school buddies, or shopping for a new pair of mittens. We design this way with good reason, of course; it only makes sense to build systems that allow people to accomplish the objectives that create a demand for those systems in the first place.

However, as discussed in Chapter 2, one of the characteristics of games is that the designers set the objectives for the players, who willingly accept those tasks because they value the experience of playing the game. By incorporating players' actions in the real world into gameplay, UX designers can gain access to people's systems of motivation and craft game experiences that will move users to action and achieve something beneficial. Importantly, this method should be applied only in cases where users already see value in taking such action but don't always have the inspiration to make it happen.

Suppose, for example, that you want people to tag images on the Web, adopt more fuel-efficient driving habits, or make micropayments to a charitable cause. Each of these tasks requires mass participation to be effective, but you can't realistically expect participation from anyone beyond the narrow minority who feel truly motivated to participate in the first place. There are even a lot of people who believe these are good things to do but lack the drive to get up and take action themselves. Without that conviction and commitment, conventional UX approaches can't succeed. Yet each of these tasks has been successfully arranged as a game experience in the real world, as I'll describe in this chapter.

This is not to say that there's anything wrong with the way interfaces are usually built. The imperative to design for existing user objectives has transformed modern software, and believe me, I am all for sticking to that approach whenever you're working with a sufficiently motivated set of users. But when you're not, game design can offer a very useful set of tools for bringing people into an experience.

This chapter focuses on an application of games that shares some similarities with how games are applied to educating and to persuading (the subjects of the next two chapters). The critical difference, however, is that games that motivate player action don't need to be concerned with transforming what people understand or believe. Instead, they are focused on the extent to which players act differently in the external world from how they would act if the game didn't exist.

Appraising a Game's Efficiency

A primary consideration for the design of a game that motivates player action is the efficiency with which playing generates solutions in the real world. Understanding this point leads to a few key questions you need to ask when you're designing a game.

- **How much will the average player be motivated to contribute?** Better designs will motivate each player to provide more work per session of play. Not that every person needs to make a substantial contribution; a small number of people who are really into the game can make up for a broader majority who engage it in passing. *Foldit*, the protein-folding game discussed in Chapter 1, puts all new players through the same set of well-trodden introductory puzzles, from which it gains no useful information. The game cannot be successful unless it has a fair number of very dedicated players.

- **How long will each player contribute?** Consider not only the time that players will spend in a single sitting, but how often they will return to the game and how long they will continue to contribute. You'll realize greater benefit from games that are played over many sittings, so allowing players to save their progress and return later should be a top priority. Better still, games that have no true ending encourage players to keep contributing until their interest naturally expires. Open-ended games like *The Sims* periodically introduce new expansions to keep players playing.

- **How many people will contribute?** The advantages you gain from maximizing the average contribution per session and the total playtime will be multiplied by the number of people playing it, so it's very important to consider whether the game you're designing has broad appeal. Remember that the point of building the game is to extend interest beyond those who were motivated to help out in the first place. Games like *Words With Friends* have appeal that cuts across multiple demographics, allowing them to include enormous numbers of players.

- **How much do I need to spend to get the desired contribution?** Create an estimate up front of the total costs of designing, developing, launching, marketing, and maintaining the game over time. Then set objectives for the benefit (contributions made, number of people signed up, number of items processed, and so on) that you need to receive to justify each dollar spent. These numbers will help drive decisions about the game's design by defining the responsibilities it needs to meet to be worthwhile. The massive overhead of technologically sophisticated games like *World of Warcraft* presents too much risk. Remember that people can find enormous satisfaction in simple games like *Bejeweled*.

Methods

Human Computation

Games that are built for human computation repurpose game interactions into useful by-products, which can be applied to tackle thorny problems in the real world. For example, *Google Image Labeler* (Figure 11.1) was designed to generate tags for Web images that have none so that they can be meaningfully indexed and searched. The game randomly pairs two people logged onto the Internet and shows both players the same image. They must then submit tags for the image, attempting to come up with the same words (they can't directly communicate with one another). When they hit on the same terms, they're both awarded points and move on to the next image. The game ends after a certain amount of time has passed, and players' scores are added to a leaderboard.

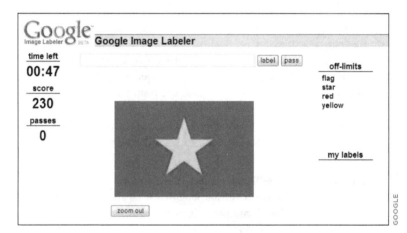

FIGURE 11.1
It's hard to describe this image without using any of the words listed in the upper right corner, unless you know that it's the flag of Vietnam.

The game's structure is intended to maximize the number of reliable tags that players submit. There's advantage in entering as many tags as come to mind, because doing that increases the probability of hitting a match before the time runs out. The tags can be considered reliable descriptions of the image because the two players, who cannot collude with each other, independently selected the same word from the entire universe of words in the English language to describe it. As a measure of reliability, the system can also match each player's tags with those submitted by other players who received the same image.

Google Image Labeler was designed by Dr. Luis von Ahn, a researcher at Carnegie Mellon University and a pioneer in human computation. He describes games as algorithms that are executed by people instead of machines. In his games, players process things that are difficult for computers to handle, such as language, images, and ideas.

Von Ahn classifies his portfolio of human computation games into three categories:

- **Output agreement.** Two players are given the same input and must find similar ways to describe it. *Google Image Labeler* is an example of an output agreement game.

- **Input agreement.** Two players need to describe to each other an object they've been given, and decide whether they were both given the same thing. *Tag a Tune*, described in the next section, is an example of an input agreement game.

- **Inversion problems.** One player is given an object and must describe it to the other player, who has to guess what it is. Password is an example of an inversion problem game.

Other Examples

Games with a Purpose

Google Image Labeler was one of several related games designed by von Ahn to demonstrate applications of human computation, which he collectively titles "games with a purpose." Other games in the series illustrate different approaches to human computation (Figure 11.2).

- *Tag a Tune.* An input agreement game in which two players listen to a music clip, describe it to each other, and then determine whether they're hearing the same music. This game produces such subjective tags as "airy," "classical," "guitar," or "rocking."

- *Verbosity.* Essentially an online version of Password, in which one player is given a term and needs to help the other player guess the term by completing phrases like "It is a type of …," "It looks like …," or "It is the opposite of …". The phrases allow the game to create output that informs ontologies cataloging the relationships between ideas.

- *Matchin.* An output agreement game in which players are shown two images and asked to pick the one they like better. Players get points when they pick the same picture. This design cleverly forces players to consider the types of images they think will appeal to other people to inform functions along the lines of Flickr's "Interestingness" filter.

- **Squigl.** A game that relies on output agreement to identify the portions of an image to which a given tag applies. Fed by results from the *ESP Game*, each player is given a noun-based tag and must draw a circle around the area of the picture in which it appears. Players receive points that reflect the extent to which their circles overlap.

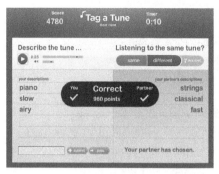

FIGURE 11.2
Other demonstrations of games designed for human computation that were developed by Luis von Ahn.

Yahoo! Answers

It's easy to think that you can find the answer to pretty much anything on the Web, but that's not really true. There are, of course, an infinite number of potential questions to be asked, which could never completely be covered by a finite (although very large) Internet. The more idiosyncratic your interest, the more likely it is that the Web hasn't yet covered it. I once wanted to know the best way to drill a straight hole for a dowel without using a jig (I didn't feel like paying for one). The answer just wasn't out there, even though there are probably a lot of people in the world who know it offhand.

Yahoo! Answers gives players a way to present those kinds of questions to people who might be able to help (Figure 11.3). After a question is submitted, the people watching the category can post their responses. People then vote on the best answers, with each vote awarding the poster a certain number of points. A bonus goes to the person voted to have submitted the best answer. As players add more answers, they level up and are ranked in a hierarchy of experts on specific subjects. Initially there's a cap on how many answers players can submit, which helps limit the volume of junk responses. But that cap lifts for individuals at higher levels, so the most reliable players can account for a greater proportion of the output.

FIGURE 11.3

Yahoo! Answers is structured to increase the chances that people will receive good answers to any question they may have.

So is *Yahoo! Answers* really a game? You bet it is. It may not present itself strongly as such, but there are objectives, constraints, rules, competition, winners, losers, rewards—all elements of a true game. Its front end takes the form of conventional Web interfaces, but its design manipulates constraints and rewards as real game elements. That design shapes a system of human computation, accepting questions as inputs and returning answers as outputs.

Best Practices for Design

The Game Experience Must Stand on Its Own

Games built for human computation have to offer players a credible game that can be enjoyed in its own right. You don't necessarily have to disguise your game's true purpose, but you do need to be concerned with what draws people to the game, and whether they're motivated to return to play it again. People might enjoy *Yahoo! Answers*, for example, because it allows them to test their competence in specific areas of knowledge or because they want to promote a social image of themselves as smarty-pants.

Bolster Quality

The quality of the output is an important consideration in the design of a human computation game because people vary in their commitment, ability, and seriousness. As a result, you must always work toward increasing the reliability of the game. One way to do this is to check results submitted independently by different people against one another. If players are registered, you will be able to see who provides the best outputs. You can then weight the work of the most reliable players more highly using systems like the leveling mechanic in *Yahoo! Answers*.

Watch Out for Cheats

Players always seek out the most efficient ways to meet a game's objectives, which may sometimes mean cheating. For example, clever players have figured out ways to make it through Luis von Ahn's *Verbosity* more quickly by using soundalikes. If the hidden word is "payment," for example, one player could send two separate hints for "pay" and "mint." This tactic corrupts the value of the game because those words aren't good descriptions of the original. When testing your game, ask players to try to figure out ways to cheat so that you can adjust your design to eliminate these loopholes.

Reframing

Games can take actions that people perform every day and frame them in a playful context that can influence actions. In contrast to human computation, these types of games give people something to work toward in the world. In order to meet objectives in the game, you must take some action in your life.

There's a lot of overlap between these games and alternate reality games, in which people play out a game fantasy in the arena of their everyday lives. The broad class of alternate reality games is beyond the scope of this book, however, because these games need not be experienced primarily through an interactive interface. Instead, I'm focusing on the subset of alternate reality games that are experienced via an app, a website, or other human-computer interaction.

Examples

Foursquare

There's a good chance that you've tried *Foursquare* by now. Its popularity has grown explosively since it was introduced at South by Southwest in March 2009. At the conference, *Foursquare* encouraged players to seek out achievements such as attending an early-morning panel or driving 25 miles outside of Austin. The game itself provided a reason to take real actions by reframing them as objectives for play.

At its heart, *Foursquare* is a location-based check-in system. It has a general sense of where you are in the world and allows you to let your friends know that you've arrived at a specific location. So say you're out barhopping and you pop into Moe's Tavern and then check into *Foursquare*. Now your friends who are next door at the comic book shop know you're around and can swing by for a Duff.

To encourage users to try new things and frequent certain locations, *Foursquare* interleaves two primary game mechanics into the experience:

- **Badges.** *Foursquare*'s badges are an achievement system that rewards players for specific actions, such as checking in four nights in a row or checking into a gym four times in a single month (Figure 11.4). Like all achievements, badges provide fantastic flexibility to create free-form objectives around just about any action. *Foursquare*'s badges gain much of their appeal from their social context, where people can see the badges their friends have managed to earn. These can make great conversation pieces when people meet up.

FIGURE 11.4
Badges in *Foursquare* have cryptic names and can be challenging to collect.

- **Mayorships.** Players who check in frequently at a particular location may be named its mayor by *Foursquare*. Some businesses have capitalized on this feature of the game by offering special privileges to their *Foursquare* mayors (Figure 11.5). This benefit gives players a motivation to seek out mayorships, bringing more business to the location.[1]

FIGURE 11.5
Special privileges, like parking spaces, can be accorded to the mayor of a given location.

COURTESY OF ERIC KLOPFER

Game elements like these are what set *Foursquare* apart. They change the system from something that allows you to document your location into something that can influence the decision to go somewhere in the first place. *Foursquare* reframes those choices as part and parcel of a game experience.

Foursquare is derided in many circles for its appropriation of gameplay to drive brand experiences. While it may have grown overly commercial, I believe it's a mistake to dismiss *Foursquare* as pure commercialism. The badges can be legitimately challenging and fun to unlock. The check-in system fosters communal experiences. Its design values gameplay, suggesting playful ways to view everyday actions. *Foursquare* would not have been able to grow to 15 million users[2] if it didn't offer intrinsically enjoyable play that people find worthwhile. Even if *Foursquare* does not represent the best way to design a reframing game, it's well worth considering the design choices that have made it so successful.

---

1 Wortham, J. (2009, October 18). Face-to-face socializing starts with a mobile post. *New York Times.* Retrieved from www.nytimes.com/2009/10/19/technology/internet/19foursquare.html.

2 Foursquare.com, last accessed December 2011.

Epic Win

Whereas *Foursquare* influences players in ways that can serve the interests of someone else, *Epic Win* encourages players to work in their own interest. Players use this iPhone app to maintain their personal to-do lists. For each task, players assign some number of experience points and a category like strength or stamina. As they cross off their to-do items, they collect the points and their personal avatars gain experience in the associated categories (Figure 11.6).

FIGURE 11.6

Epic Win adopts the aesthetic conventions of games to reframe to-do items as quests that advance players within a game world.

Epic Win reframes any mundane task players may have—washing the dishes, filling out a tax return, or finishing a wireframe—as a game challenge and as a fantasy. As players earn more experience, their avatars move forward along a road, periodically collecting objects—which are often very funny—along the way (Figure 11.7). This is a variable-ratio schedule, which, as you'll recall from Chapter 9, is associated with the fastest rate of response. The player's character also levels up after earning a set number of experience points, increasing the frequency with which they find objects.

FIGURE 11.7
Players periodically level up and unlock new items from a large collection, each of which comes with a funny description. This is a nested reward system.

Could players cheat? Sure. The system has no way of monitoring whether people have actually completed their tasks or whether the tasks were legitimate in the first place. But cheating would make the experience pointless. By bringing their lives into *Epic Win*, players collaborate with the designers to enable the game experience.

HiveMind

In late 2011, Will Wright, designer of games like *The Sims*, started dropping tantalizing hints that his new venture in development, *HiveMind*, will be a radical sophistication on reframing games like these. Details remain sketchy as of publication, but Wright has described *HiveMind* as creating custom game experiences for individuals based on multiple dimensions of information it gathers about them. He describes it this way: "Rather than craft a game like *FarmVille* for players to learn and play, we learn about you and your routines and incorporate that into a form of game play."[3] Of course, the proof of the game is in the playing, but given *HiveMind*'s pedigree, it's well worth paying attention to its progress.

---

3 Takahashi, D. (2011, November 16). *Inside Will Wright's next big game: HiveMind.* GamesBeat. Retrieved from www.venturebeat.com/2011/11/16/will-wright-hivemind.

Best Practices for Design

Make It Easy to Play Along

Reframing games depend on people bouncing between life and the game to keep track of their progress. The player has to be willing to revisit the game world over and over again to get information, report progress, and stay inside the experience. It's no coincidence, then, that these types of games tend to find homes on mobile platforms.

To the extent that you can make each interaction as easy as possible for the player, you'll encourage greater participation. Work to minimize the amount of time it takes to open the application, interact with it, and get back to real life. Make the most frequently used features the most efficient ones to access when the player first opens the app. Use any available location-based or time-based information to preselect options for the player. For example, *Foursquare* uses geopositioning to serve up a short list of nearby places to visit.

Create an Alternate Existence

Games that reframe the player's real-world actions benefit by crafting a more tangible alternate reality that runs parallel to life. Players are simultaneously living in two worlds, and both should be interesting. *Epic Win*, for example, creates a strong element of fantasy by using the medieval themes common to role-playing games. Not all themes will appeal to all people, so it's beneficial to allow players to select a custom motif—science fiction or western, for example. *Foursquare* is not fantastical, but it nonetheless has its own false reality of mayorships and fictional merit badges.

Focus on Varied and Fresh Rewards

Well-crafted reward systems can provide players with compelling reasons to play. But remember that not all reward systems appeal to every player in the same way. Leaderboards, for example, may not appeal to people who don't like viewing the experience competitively, and other people might view item collections as trite. So mix it up; give people multiple ways to play and enjoy the experience. The more types of rewards you offer, the greater is the possibility that players will take an interest in one of them.

Because players need to revisit the game frequently, it's also helpful to reinforce the feeling that they're making progress. Provide rewards often enough that players feel they're getting somewhere and that the return visits are meaningful. Also provide enough new rewards to sustain player interest over time. *Epic Win* offers many dozens of objects and promises to add completely new reward systems to the game over time. This kind of open-ended approach to rewards helps keep the experience from going stale.

Real-Time Reinforcement

Some games expand on the basic reframing method by providing continual feedback to players as they go about a particular activity, allowing them to see how they're doing as they're doing it. Feedback is useful when you want to help players get better at something, or when you want to provide a motivation to try something new.

Examples

Honda Insight Eco Assist

The rate at which a car consumes fuel depends on two factors: the efficiency of the vehicle and the way it's driven. Solutions to improving fuel economy have traditionally focused on the hardware, perhaps assuming that you can't engineer the way people drive. However, the Eco Assist system in Honda's Insight hybrid car uses a game to alter people's ingrained driving habits (get there fast, zoom out in front, stop hard) and reframe driving as a quest to save gas.

The background of the car's speedometer changes color from blue to green when the driver is exercising more fuel-efficient driving habits. This is real-time feedback, allowing the driver to discover which actions guzzle fuel and avoid those maneuvers in the future. If the speedometer remains green for a certain period, then a group of virtual plants begins to grow in the middle of the dashboard (Figure 11.8). Drivers are awarded trophies for successfully growing all of the plants.

This feedback system boosts the car's fuel efficiency beyond what can be achieved through mechanical engineering alone.

FIGURE 11.8
The dashboard of the Honda Insight hybrid incorporates a simple plant-growing game into the driving experience to give people feedback about the fuel efficiency of their driving habits.

The Pokéwalker

Two versions of *Pokémon* for the Nintendo DS come bundled with a pedometer called the Pokéwalker (Figure 11.9). Players can increase their monster's health by wearing the device as they walk, run, and exercise. They can then sync the Pokéwalker to the game saved on the cartridge the next time they play.

FIGURE 11.9
Worn on the belt, the Pokéwalker overlays a game experience on the real world, so that taking a walk becomes an action within the game world itself.

NINTENDO

The Pokéwalker extends the game fantasy into real life. Players select an imaginary course to walk that's themed to locations in the game world, such as "Dim Cave" and "Blue Lake." As they take walks in the real world, they are also walking through these locations in the virtual world. The Pokéwalker alerts them periodically when, in this parallel game universe, they come across a monster to capture or a useful item like a potion. The more steps players take, the more game rewards they collect. This fixed-interval reinforcement schedule encourages players to exercise more vigorously to maximize the benefits they gain within the game.

Nike+

The Nike+ system that's now integrated into iPods and iPhones similarly tracks exercise in progress and reframes it. Using either GPS or a sensor placed inside a Nike shoe, runners hear periodic updates on their progress through their iPod. As players reach new personal bests, they're rewarded with prerecorded congratulations from Nike-signed athletes like Lance

Armstrong and Paula Radcliffe. Players also earn points called CardioMiles that are based on the number of calories they've burned. In addition, Nike+ creates competition by allowing players to upload all their data to an online profile, where they can create challenges and routes for their friends to run.

Best Practices for Design

Because real-time reinforcement is a sophistication of reframing, all of the best practices noted in our earlier discussion of reframing apply here, along with the following design considerations specific to this approach.

Specialize

Real-time reinforcement is more effective when it can run alongside a narrow task the player is completing, rather than a broad set of actions. It's not practical to shadow and detect a person's every movement. Instead, specializing the game to measure a few actions that are instrumental to a real-world objective can be cost-effective while providing useful guidance to the player.

The Honda Insight Eco Assist system is a good example. Its sensors are directly hardwired into the car's systems, and they detect each instance of braking or acceleration. A more general system that just reported the usage of gasoline over distance would not be as effective at addressing the driving habits affecting gasoline consumption.

Take Advantage of Reinforcement Schedules

Because you're detecting the player's actions as they're in progress, you have a great opportunity to shape the way players execute those actions. Recall from Chapter 9 that different schedules of reinforcement create different effects. Continuous reinforcement works best when new behaviors are first being learned. Variable-ratio schedules produce the fastest rate of response. Fixed-interval schedules produce a burst of activity just around the time that a reward is expected. Consider the effects you want to achieve, and select the schedules that best support them.

Optional Advantages

A different way to fiddle with people's objectives is to present real-world actions as optional advantages in the game. If players choose not to partake, they'll still have an acceptable experience, but the game creates an incentive for them to take action to get something above and beyond the normal game experience. This strategy can provide a very strong motivation to players who are really into a game, because it can offer more efficient ways for them to meet their game objectives.

Examples

Game developer Zynga has demonstrated real mastery of this method by giving players the option to take real-world actions to improve their competitive position in a game.

CityVille

Like other Zynga games, *CityVille* is designed to elicit many small payments from players over time. Optional advantages are made available through a virtual currency of coins and cash, which players can purchase using real money (Figure 11.10). Players can also get game money by placing orders through affiliated businesses, providing an alternative revenue stream through advertisers. Such is the wonderful flexibility of a virtual currency: there are many ways to get it, and many ways to use it.

FIGURE 11.10
Players have the option to make their progress in *CityVille* easier by paying real money to buy virtual currency. But they don't have to.

Cash in particular gives players access to multiple, very attractive shortcuts in the game. For example, players need to convince Facebook friends to volunteer to fill positions at community buildings like clinics and police stations in order for those facilities to open. If the player can't persuade enough friends to sign up, then for a small amount of cash they can hire game characters to fill the empty spots. Either way, Zynga wins; you're either paying them money or bringing other people into the game who could also pay them money.

Cash can also be used to gain access to locked content such as houses and businesses, allowing the player to move the game forward more quickly. This is a form of negative reinforcement that relieves players of some tedium if they grow impatient with the game's progress.

In no case are players forced to contribute real money, but the game builds powerful motivations to do so by offering advantages in the gameplay experience.

Zynga Charitable Initiatives

Generating corporate revenue isn't the only reason to use optional advantages; they can also serve altruistic social ends. One way to gain *CityVille* cash, for example, is to make a donation to a charitable organization such as the United Way.

Through games, charitable organizations can raise a lot of money by offering inexpensive rewards that donors highly value. After the earthquake that devastated Haiti in 2010, Zynga launched an initiative offering white corn seeds to *FarmVille* players (Figure 11.11). The special crop had everything going for it: it granted players a large number of experience points, it was lucrative, it could be harvested in a very short time, and it would never wither and die like other *FarmVille* crops if it was left untended. Players had to pay real money to buy the corn, but all proceeds went to Haiti relief. The feature cost Zynga virtually nothing to create, and it raised $1 million in donations in five days.

FIGURE 11.11
FarmVille players were given the opportunity to buy a special crop, the proceeds from which were given to Haiti relief.

Best Practices for Design

Build Investment in the Experience

For an optional advantage to work, players must first understand its value. Such appreciation can only come from developing a sense of the underlying game and becoming invested in the experience. There are a few good ways to do this:

- **Remove all barriers to entry.** It can be hard to persuade people that they should shell out money up front to play a game they haven't tried. But if you let them try your game for free, you can give them the opportunity to become invested in the experience and decide whether it's worth paying for additional advantages.

- **Give players a sense of ownership in the game world.** Allow players to create custom characters, properties, and other things that are uniquely their own. *CityVille* does this masterfully. In everything from naming the city and its businesses to placing each building, you know that this place is completely yours.

- **Give players a sense of incomplete progress toward long-term objectives.** *FarmVille* players get to plant their seeds in one visit, but nothing comes of it until they come back hours or days later. Letting players do some work in the game that can't be finished right away is an effective way to build interest, because it invites the impression that the initial effort will be in vain if they don't return.

Keep Options Optional

Keep in mind that some proportion of players will not take advantage of the optional advantage on offer. If this means they will eventually hit a wall and not be able to make any more progress without giving you something in return, then opting out means abandoning the experience. Through attrition, the player community will diminish over time. If, instead of opting out, these people could contribute but still stay in the game, they might choose to opt in later. So always provide another way to get the job done and keep players playing, which may simply mean that players need to put in more time or effort or that they aren't given access to the same privileges as the players who opt in.

Create Disproportionate Rewards...

The greater the contrast between what players are asked to give and what they receive in return, the more compelling the option's value proposition is. Because the game world is entirely virtual, great rewards can be very cost-effective. As the designer, you can grant the player extraordinary power, control, or luxury in return for a modest contribution if it costs you almost nothing to create those things.

People who contributed to the *FarmVille* Haiti relief campaign, for example, were treated to an extra bonus on the day it ended: they all received an energy bar that, once consumed, greatly increased their characters' speed for a full day. Speed is tremendously valuable in *FarmVille*, because it reduces the time required to plant and harvest crops (a negative reinforcement), which, depending on the size of the player's farm, can be very long indeed. Players who got the bonus received a tremendous one-day advantage.

...but Don't Allow Cheating

In a competitive or social game, there's a danger that paying to play can be seen as creating unfair advantages for those who opt in. The line is hazy, but there is a difference between an acceptable paid advantage and a cheat, and crossing that line can breed resentment. Be especially careful to avoid anything that upsets the power symmetry among players. If you're hosting a game in which players enter skirmishes with one another, for example, giving one player complete invincibility to any attack would go too far. If players can win because they paid for the privilege, the experience is cheapened for everyone.

Scheduled Play

Designers can use game mechanics to encourage players to revisit websites and apps on a regular basis by offering scheduled opportunities for play, increasing the stickiness of those experiences. Between specified times in the schedule, play doesn't happen, which builds anticipation for the next opportunity. This method can be an inexpensive way to motivate users to return regularly, while injecting a small element of thrill into an everyday experience.

Examples

Amazon Gold Box

The Gold Box has become a familiar fixture on Amazon's website, offering discounts on merchandise that are revealed periodically. Over time, it has evolved from a single item each day to a fixed-interval hourly countdown of items organized around a theme. The regularity of the schedule encourages visits to the site.

The Gold Box uses elements of uncertainty to build interest in the deal of the moment. Each day, the Gold Box lists semicryptic hints about each item that will go on sale (Figure 11.12). The exact item and the size of the discount remain unknown. The prospect of what might be revealed is often more compelling than the thing itself.

FIGURE 11.12
Amazon's Gold Box
gives users a reason
to check in regularly
to find out what deals
have become available.

Once the Gold Box deal is announced, two countdowns begin. The first shows the time remaining before the deal expires, and the second shows the number of discounts remaining. Both create a sense of scarcity and urgency.

CityVille Daily Bonus

CityVille's daily bonus rewards players for returning to the game on consecutive days. Each day that players return and help out a neighbor, they receive larger and larger payouts in *CityVille* coins. After playing for five days in a row, players are given a chance to win a special property. If they skip a day, they start the daily bonus over again. By giving away things that have no real-world value in exchange for participating, *CityVille* is able to effectively boost community activity at no expense to itself.

Best Practices for Design

Validate the Schedule through Testing

How often is it reasonable to ask players to return to a game? For some proportion of players, return visits are not practical under any circumstances. Within the remaining community, the appropriate frequency varies. If the schedule requires more frequent visits than most people can realistically handle, participation will dwindle and fade.

Ideally, you should require the fewest number of return visits that the largest number of players will actually honor. The only way to reliably project this number is to pilot-test the game with different settings. Splitting the test into multiple threads allows you to evaluate different scenarios simultaneously (several times a day, once a day, once a week, or any other variation) and quickly discover the ones that will maximize participation. If the sample sizes are large enough to be statistically significant, you can expect the behavior you see on the small scale to hold true when those settings are generalized to the full player population.

The appropriate frequency may also change over time as the novelty of the experience wears off. Consider adapting the schedule once a player's participation begins to falter.

Apart from the required frequency of play, the other major factor influencing the decision of players to revisit an experience is the perceived value of the reward they'll receive for doing so.

You can use the fact that you're working in a virtual world to your advantage by giving away things that cost nearly nothing for you to create. But don't overdo the generosity either. A reward that gives the player too much of an advantage simply for showing up can drain the challenge from the game. Even worse, lavishing people with grand door prizes can lead players to view them as entitlements rather than as rewards given in exchange for a particular action.

There are various types of tactics you can use to avoid these destructive cycles:

- **Graduated.** As in *CityVille*, build up from smaller to greater rewards as the player returns to the experience on successive occasions.

- **Probabilistic.** Make the reward a chance to win a prize, rather than just giving something away. Reward higher rates of participation with greater probabilities of winning.

- **Competitive.** Let players compete against one another, so that those who revisit first or most frequently claim the best rewards, and progressively weaker rewards go to those who follow.

Different Is Good

The strategies described in this chapter are not what most UX designers are accustomed to, but they are also no longer unusual. User experiences that influence the motivations of the people using them, rather than just supporting the motivations they already have when they arrive at the experience, are now plentiful. I firmly believe that such designs will only become more commonplace as designers become more familiar with their advantages and master their best practices.

Tools that motivate player's external actions can be great additions to the UX designer's tool kit. In the next two chapters I'll explore how games can be used to transform people from the inside out.

CHAPTER 12

Games for Learning

Historically, games have long had a presence in education, from classroom exercises like spelling bees and geography-themed bingo to academic competitions like debating clubs and Model UN. It shouldn't be terribly surprising, then, that some successful video game franchises have focused on learning and been welcomed in schools:

- *The Oregon Trail.* A classic game originally created in 1971 that simulated pioneer life in the 1840s and presented lessons in history and ecology.

- *Where in the World Is Carmen Sandiego?* A series of mystery-themed video games that taught geography.

- *Math Blaster.* A space adventure game that drilled mathematics.

Developers of educational video games have traditionally taken an approach that some people have compared to chocolate-covered broccoli—applying a thin game veneer to material that is recognizably unaltered from traditional classroom lessons. There's a certain cynicism in this way of thinking that doesn't highly regard either education or games. It implies that education is an inherently unpleasant thing and that no enjoyment is to be found in subjects like math, geography, science, or literature in and of themselves. It also implies that the role of educational games is to obscure the actual educational activity so that learners are more willing to bear the unpleasantness of learning. In addition, the quality of the player experience in such games has often been sacrificed in service to educational objectives.

In recent years, researchers, educators, and game designers have explored new ways to use games for education and training, for both children and adults, and have even transformed traditional models of learning through gameplay. In the modern view, games have unique attributes that can enable means of learning that aren't otherwise easily available. These attributes create opportunities for UX designers to create compelling learning systems.

Even a game built purely for entertainment can demand tremendous effort from players to learn how to succeed at it. *Civilization V*, for example, in which players must build and manage societies spanning all of human history, presents well-structured learning that players acquire voluntarily (Figure 12.1). The game also creates an opportunity to reflect on human history and to experiment with both the internal and external factors that lead to the rise and fall of different regimes.[1]

Games like *Civilization V* can add an entirely new mode of learning to traditional means of instruction—one that can form a very effective complement to textbooks and lectures. This viewpoint assigns games a

---

1 Shaffer, D. W., Squire, K. D., Halverson, R., & Gee, J. P. (2005). Video games and the future of learning. *Phi Delta Kappan*, *87*, 105–111.

much more sophisticated role in learning than they have traditionally occupied, and it finds an intrinsic joy in learning for its own sake. Designers creating games for learning today should build experiences that marry subject matter to people's innate fascination with new ideas.

This chapter explores how UX designers can make use of the unique advantages that games create for learning. First I review the qualities of games that make them suited to learning. Then I discuss specific ways in which designers are using games in learning environments. Much of the current work being done focuses on children, but the basic principles generalize well to any audience and can be repurposed for professional training, customer education, or awareness programs.

FIGURE 12.1
In *Civilization V*, history is a game.

What Makes Games Suited to Learning?

There's something of a cultural bias against video games, regarding them as anti-intellectual pursuits that numb their players' brains and offer no meaningful gain in knowledge. In fact, video games have certain inherent advantages that make them powerful tools for facilitating learning, often in ways that are difficult to accomplish by other means.

Advantages to Learners

Agency and Mastery

One of the reasons learners become discouraged is that they lack a feeling of *agency*, or personal control over outcomes. When people come to believe that the learning process is outside of their control, they may give up on learning altogether. Some children think they cannot succeed in math class, and many adults feel powerless when trying to use a computer, for example.

Video game players, on the other hand, are entrusted with the responsibility of being fully in charge of something, giving them complete control over outcomes. Games thus create a strong sense that winning and losing are within the player's power. They also give players the ability to structure the experience themselves, learning what they need to know as they need to know it. The player is in a position of power, which can be a valuable role for learners who lack a sense of power in real life.

Furthermore, the process of becoming competent with any game requires players to gain *mastery* over a domain of knowledge, promoting a feeling of ownership of the subject matter. In many games, success is directly tied to the player's depth of understanding of the game world. Putting players in competition with one another can increase the drive to master the domain, so that the players really have to know their stuff in order to win.

The PC strategy game *Sins of a Solar Empire* illustrates principles of both agency and mastery in games (Figure 12.2). Each player commands an entire fleet of space vessels locked in an interplanetary struggle for dominance. The fate of the fleet rises and falls with the player's choices; no one is preempting the player's control over the outcome. People playing *Sins of a Solar Empire* must also learn the intricacies of its universe, such as its 45 different types of space vessels and the unique strengths, weaknesses, behaviors, and alliances of each. Substituting spaceships for cells and tissues, a very similar game could be used to teach anatomy and physiology, and to demonstrate how the body defends itself against disease and infection.

Failure-Based Learning

Will Wright, designer of *The Sims* and *SimCity*, coined the phrase "failure-based learning" in reference to the way games allow players the latitude to fail and fail again until they get it right. In this view, failure is an essential part of the learning process, which is a departure from the traditional view of failure as proof that no learning has occurred.[2]

---

2 Corbett, S. (2010, September 19). Learning by playing: Video games in the classroom. *New York Times Magazine*.

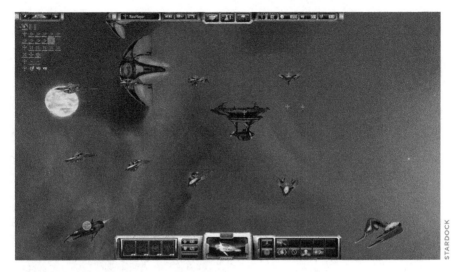

FIGURE 12.2
Players need to master the complexities of managing their own personal space armada to succeed in *Sins of a Solar Empire*.

Two key characteristics of games make them well suited to supporting failure-based learning:

- Players appreciate the unwritten rule that games are designed in such a way that success is always possible, even if it's very difficult.

- There are no permanent consequences of failing—only temporary setbacks. So games give players every reason to try and try again.

Failure-based learning offers people the opportunity to understand their failures better, inviting a cycle of critical thinking and problem solving. To increase their chances of success the next time around, learners need to try first, then analyze why what they tried didn't work, then develop hypotheses about how they can minimize those factors, then try something new, and so on. Failure is an indispensable part of this process because it brings learners closer to the right answers by exposing problems in their reasoning and creating the opportunity to correct those problems.

Failure-based learning also teaches players the important life lesson that you don't need to feel paralyzed by failure. When something doesn't work, just regroup, change your approach, and give it another go. This is a very pragmatic way of learning because it reflects how many things actually get done in the real world. In UX design, we go through multiple iterations of design and testing before rolling out a product because we expect that some things won't work. Relatively few difficult challenges can be overcome on the first try. When people don't develop a tolerance for failure, they limit their potential for success.

Video games are a wonderful way to acclimate people to failure and to help them develop the skills needed to surmount difficult challenges. *Angry Birds* provides a great example (Figure 12.3). The objective of each of the hundreds of levels in the game is the same: to destroy the malevolent green pigs by using a slingshot to hurl different types of birds into the pigs' fortresses of stone, wood, and ice. Players are given a limited number of birds to throw, and they must determine how to use the specific attributes of each type of bird to attack the unique construction of each fortress. *Angry Birds* is a model of failure-based learning because players almost always need to try each level several times. With each try they come to understand the problem a little bit better—discovering weaknesses in the fortress's structure and better tactics for using each of their birds. As soon as the player finally succeeds, a new challenge is presented and the process starts over again. Players spend much more time failing in *Angry Birds* than they do succeeding.

FIGURE 12.3
I played this level in *Angry Birds* a good 30 times before finally clearing it. Each time, I learned a little bit more about what works and what doesn't.

Algebra Touch for the iPhone is a game that asks players to solve increasingly difficult equations as new structures or axioms are added at each level (Figure 12.4). Each problem is solvable, no matter how difficult, and players are free to fail as many times as they need to before arriving at the correct solution. The core mechanic of *Algebra Touch* is, in fact, not entirely dissimilar from that of *Angry Birds*. In both games, players need to understand the unique properties of the elements provided to them, and then must use these elements to reduce a structured object to a simpler state. Both games enable failure-based learning, allowing players the latitude to keep trying until they get it right.

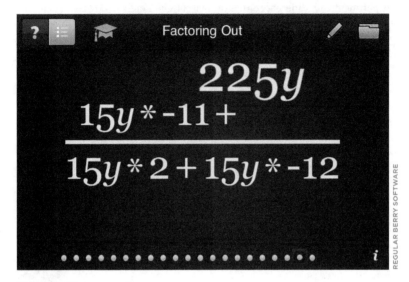

FIGURE 12.4
In *Algebra Touch*, players manipulate equations by dragging and dropping. With each move, they learn a little bit more about what works and what doesn't.

Learning by Doing

Video games give learners the opportunity to gain hands-on experience with the things that they're learning about. Because they face no real-world consequences, players are free to ask "What if…?" and explore the boundaries of a game space to see what happens under different circumstances. In this way, games encourage a spirit of inquiry and exploration. Similarly, early versions of Microsoft Office came with very useful built-in tutorials that allowed users to learn how to use the applications by working through examples. The help system in recent versions has taken a big step down by replacing these active hands-on learning systems with straight copy and passive videos.

Importantly, games can closely mirror the conditions of the real world without putting any real-world objects at risk. Although you wouldn't give students unsupervised control of a real chemistry lab, there's no downside to letting them blow up a simulated one. Games can give players access to things that would be too expensive, impractical, or unsafe for them to use in the real world. *Flight Simulator*, for example, lets players get practical experience flying a plane without any of the risks.

The Incredible Machine for the iPad is one such virtual lab. It allows players to experiment with different configurations of Rube Goldberg devices to achieve a stated objective (Figure 12.5). When the completed device is run, objects fly around the screen following the laws of physics (though in two dimensions). There are many possible paths to success, so players need to use ingenuity and experiment with the utility of devices ranging from catapults to rockets.

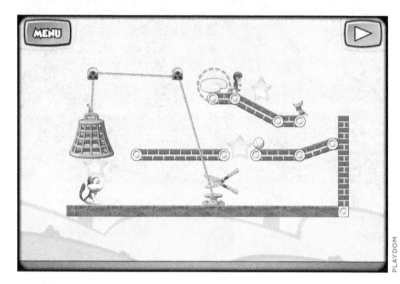

PLAYDOM

FIGURE 12.5

In the process of playing *The Incredible Machine*, players learn a lot about basic physics, including the laws of motion, gravity, and energy.

There's some controversy about whether education is more effective when a teacher tells and then shows, or shows and then tells. To some extent, students need background knowledge to make sense of an experiment, but it's also much easier to learn the theory behind something after they've had some experience with how it works.[3] Some research indicates that students get the most out of a hybrid approach in which they move freely between theory and experience.[4] It's easy to imagine interactive e-books being developed that integrate theory and practice by interspersing small interactive games to illustrate particular points throughout the text.

3   Gee, J. P. (2007). *What video games have to teach us about learning and literacy.* New York, NY: Palgrave Macmillan, p. 114.

4   Klopfer, E. (2011, June). *An ecologist's perspective on the ecology of learning games.* Keynote address presented at the Games+Learning+Society Conference in Madison, WI.

Role Playing

Learners can be inhibited by an inability to imagine putting the things they're studying to productive use in their own lives. Studying astronomy makes sense if you can see yourself becoming an astronomer, but if not, then the time spent learning about it can seem pointless. Games can be valuable in this regard because they encourage players to try on different identities, giving them the opportunity to imagine themselves as scientists, managers, or titans of industry. This kind of role playing can create aspirational targets for self-development.

Learning-game theorist James Paul Gee[5] proposes that games support role playing through what he calls the "projective identity," which is neither the player nor the player's in-game character, but the player's vision of who his or her in-game character should be. Players take actions in the game consistent with their vision of who the game character should become. For example, *The Sims* allows players to create many characters, but without projective identities they're just empty shells. Players must decide whether they want a character to be a supportive nurturer, a steadfast breadwinner, or an incorrigible playboy (Figure 12.6). The projective identities invite players to reflect on what they value or don't value. In constructing these personas, players also try on different worldviews.

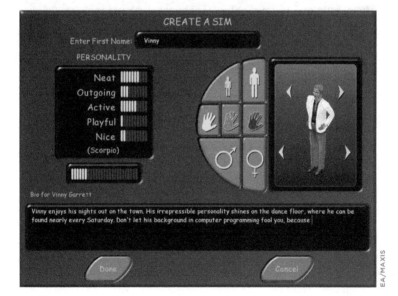

FIGURE 12.6
The user interface in *The Sims* encourages players to construct rich projective identities.

---

5 Gee, *What video games have to teach us*, p. 50.

A game could equivalently put players in the role of an astronomer, and let the players make decisions that would affect their career trajectory. Players would need to construct a projective identity for the character, think about what they would value in such a person, and then select the character's actions accordingly. In the process, players must ask, "What would I do if I were an astronomer?"

If a game is being designed with the intention of encouraging players to try on a different role, then it's important to give players options to customize their characters so that they feel they're involved in constructing the projective identity. Many games invite this kind of customization by allowing players to:

- Customize an avatar's physical appearance so that players can model their character after themselves, their role models, or other people they know.

- Select the fundamental attributes of a game character—charisma, intelligence, strength, and so on. Many games give players a limited number of points to distribute among such attributes, forcing them to make choices about the things they really value. A game designed to develop people management skills, for example, could give players a set number of points to allocate to personality traits like nurturing, autocratic, and optimistic. These character attributes could create interesting scenarios when juxtaposed with in-game characters who have different values for dependability, autonomy, and efficiency.

- Exercise meaningful choices about their characters' in-game behavior. Players should not be constrained to a single narrow path dictated by the game's designers, but be free to choose from a variety of different courses. For example, *Star Wars: Knights of the Old Republic* provides very different gameplay experiences and outcomes depending on whether players make decisions that lead them down the light side or the dark side of the Force, and in turn change the course of the game's narrative. There is no preferred outcome; it comes down to what the player desires for the character. Continuing the management game example, a similar mechanic could translate into choices that lead people to reflect on management styles that could work for them, and strategies for handling difficult situations.

Advantages for Training and Instruction

Built-in Assessment

Games present an entirely new way to handle testing. The game itself can serve as the assessment of a person's performance. Game-based tests can provide a different model for evaluating success—one in which learners are allowed to retry as many times as necessary to complete the game's objectives. What matters is the outcome—whether a person has mastered the subject matter or acquired the skill set needed to complete objectives in the game. Applied to a classroom environment or training systems, differentiation between students' grades can be based on the total number of objectives completed, the difficulties of each of those objectives, and the quality or speed with which they were done.

For example, a game designed to teach anatomy may require the player to build a functioning circulatory system for a fictional creature. If the player can't get the blood flowing properly through the heart, lungs, and tissues of the body, then the creature can't come to life and the player cannot advance in the game. Once the creature is up and running, the suitability of the circulatory system that the player constructed for that creature could determine its health, and better health could equate to a higher grade for the assignment.

Assessing achievement in this way also gives players the chance to reflect on their own satisfaction with their performance, and to put in additional effort before submitting their results for a final grade. This design further capitalizes on the sense of agency that games naturally create.

Scaffolding and Differentiation

Games can provide an automated way of tailoring instruction to the individual needs, strengths, and interests of different learners, creating scaffolding that gives each player the level of support needed. Those who need greater support can be given additional guidance and be routed into more detailed tutorials that focus on the specific difficulties they're having with the subject matter. If they need more practice, the game can dynamically adjust the number of levels they need to complete before moving on. For learners who demonstrate competence quickly, those same tutorials and levels can be compressed or skipped to prevent them from becoming bored and frustrated.

Games can also differentiate instruction for different learners by allowing them to pursue their individual interests and use the skills that come naturally to them. For example, a multiplayer game might depend on some players using mathematics to calculate the efficiency of a car engine, other players conducting research to identify the advantages of different engine designs, and still others using computer-assisted design software to improve the engine's efficiency. All are learning about the design of car engines, but a structure like this one gives each player the chance to be successful in a different way. As a final exercise, engines designed by the different player teams could be placed into identical virtual cars and raced against one another to demonstrate which players have the best command of the underlying concepts.

Higher-Order Thinking

In a 2006 paper, the Federation of American Scientists reported that many video games on the commercial market, by nature of their design, give players practice in building higher-order skills that are vital to a 21st-century economy.[6] Games can impart these skills with an efficiency that isn't easy for educators to achieve by other means. In this way, video games can play a unique role in preparing learners to think in a variety of ways that will create long-term value for themselves and for society.

Strategic Thinking

Many games require players to plan their moves several steps ahead, and to select short-term tactics that will support their long-term strategies. This design is common in games that fall into the real-time strategy genre, which give players concentrated practice in analyzing a situation, formulating possible actions, visualizing outcomes, and adapting to change. These skills are certainly valuable in fighting wars, but no less so in activism, politics, business, law, or diplomacy.

Age of Empires III, for example, couches such strategic challenges in the context of hypothetical wars between European colonial powers in the New World (Figure 12.7). Players cannot succeed through brute force, by charging ahead and attacking mindlessly. Instead, for each battle scenario they need to think through the movement of their available forces in advance. They need to decide which units should move ahead, which should pull back, and which should engage the opposition's troops. The game also requires players to shift strategies dynamically as the battle evolves, and then adapt again as the time period advances and industrialization demands an entirely new calculus. It's not difficult to imagine a training game that would use similar structures to teach business strategy and adaptability in an evolving market.

Systems Thinking

Video games can model complex systems with many interacting parts, and drop players right in the middle of those spinning gears. This capability gives players the opportunity to understand and manipulate the dynamic relationships between a whole and its parts. Areas of study such as ecology, sociology, and information technology all require a core aptitude in systems thinking, and games can be a great way to teach it.

This kind of modeling has always been the hallmark of simulation games. One of the first in this genre was *Utopia*, a game for the Intellivision home system in 1982. In it, two players compete against one another by managing

---

6 Federation of American Scientists. (2006). *Harnessing the power of video games for learning.* Summit on Educational Games. Washington, DC: FAS, p. 20, www.fas.org/gamesummit/Resources/Summit%20on%20Educational%20Games.pdf.

the social and economic development of separate islands (Figure 12.8). They take turns constructing different items. Farms provide food and income for the island's population. Factories provide more income but increase social discontent through pollution. Schools, hospitals, and housing improve social happiness and increase the productivity of factories, but they're costly to build and maintain. The players continually face threats from pirates, home-grown rebellions, and hurricanes. They can mount defenses by building forts and purchasing PT boats, but at the risk of further alienating the population. To succeed, players need to master the complex relationships between the moving parts while keeping an eye on the effects their actions have on the island as a whole.

MICROSOFT GAME STUDIOS

FIGURE 12.7
Age of Empires III forces players to think strategically and adapt quickly to shifting battlefield conditions.

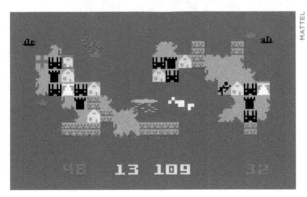

MATTEL

FIGURE 12.8
Despite its boxy appearance, *Utopia* is a game of remarkable sophistication that incorporates systems thinking into its core mechanic.

The environmental constraints of a video game can be designed to teach players how to work most productively in situations when they're short on resources or time—a relevant skill in almost any job. Many games are fundamentally about figuring out the most efficient way to get a job done.

All of the games in the *Resident Evil* series, for example, give the player a very limited amount of ammunition to fight off the zombies that have taken over a city. Players also periodically come across medicinal plants that, when mixed together, can have different effects, from restoring health to neutralizing poison. Importantly, all resources are expended when they're used, and players are at risk of running out if they haven't used them efficiently. Players must make calculated trade-offs to keep the game moving.

Sticking with the undead theme, *Plants vs. Zombies* challenges players to effectively construct a machine that runs at peak efficiency (Figure 12.9). As waves of zombies approach the house, the player needs to make defensive decisions that will keep them from making it all the way to the door. A variety of plants available to the player can kill zombies, slow them down, or provide the energy needed to grow more plants, but they can be placed in the ground only every so often. The time to make decisions is further limited by the inexorable advance of the zombies, forcing the player to make the most of what's available at any given moment. In its ideal state, the player's garden will continually keep the zombies at bay without the player's active control, requiring only occasional maintenance to replace plants that have been damaged in battle. Getting there requires a level of critical thinking that continually evaluates the efficiency of the machine.

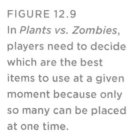

FIGURE 12.9
In *Plants vs. Zombies*, players need to decide which are the best items to use at a given moment because only so many can be placed at one time.

James Paul Gee

There is something of a rage these days for game-based learning in and out of schools. What I have always found interesting about video games, most certainly including commercial games, is the many ways in which they "teach."

- First, they focus on well-ordered problems, not just facts and information.

- Second, they give players good tools with which to solve the problems (including the help of other players in multiplayer gaming, and facts and information as tools).

- Third, they have clear goals but, nonetheless, encourage players to rethink their goals from time to time.

- Fourth, they lower the cost of failure so that players will explore, take risks, seek alternative solutions, and try new styles of play and learning.

- Fifth, they put performance before competence and they put experiences and actions before words and texts. This means that players learn by doing and that they have images and experiences to give deep meaning to the words and texts they read later as resources for their play and learning.

- Sixth, games give copious feedback, and they make constant assessments to ensure that the player is always well prepared for what comes next.

- Seventh, they connect playing and learning to social interaction and mentoring through collaborative and competitive play, as well as through interest-driven fan sites where players can extend and articulate their knowledge and even produce new knowledge and designs.

- Eighth, they ensure that at each new level, players face new problems that challenge the routine mastery they have developed through lots of practice on the previous levels (this has been called the "cycle of expertise").

- Ninth, they use narrative in two ways to create engagement: (1) They often have stories that make clear why the players are doing what they're doing and what it means, and (2) they allow players to create their own stories through the consequential choices they have made in the course of gameplay.

- Tenth, they hold everyone to the same high standard (everyone, for example, fights the same "bosses"), but allow players to reach these standards in different ways and in different amounts of time (so it doesn't really matter where or when one started, only where one finishes).

sidebar continues on next page

- Eleventh, they deal with transfer as "preparation for future learning." You can see how well players have learned by seeing how well they do in similar later and harder games or problems in life.

- Twelfth, to play a game successfully, gamers have to think like designers, because they have to figure out how the "rule system" in the game works and how it can be used to accomplish their goals. They can go further and "mod" the game (make new levels or versions) using the design software with which the game was made.

Such teaching through good design is pervasive in out-of-school learning today for all ages. It could someday, too, become the foundation for real school reform.

James Paul Gee is the Mary Lou Fulton Presidential Professor of Literary Studies at Arizona State University. He has written several books exploring the educational capacity of video games, including What Video Games Have to Teach Us About Learning and Literacy *and* Good Video Games and Good Learning.

Strategies for Using Games to Support Learning

Utilizing the advantages just discussed, contemporary designers are inventing novel approaches to games to support learning. Several patterns are emerging from these efforts, as are best practices that UX designers can adopt to guide implementations of such games.

To Impart Content

The most traditional application of learning games is as a vehicle for directly communicating subject matter. In this model the game's purpose is to teach the embedded concepts using a format that's fun and engaging. In this way the game can be overtly tied to an educational curriculum but create the opportunity for people to learn the subject from the inside as active participants rather than as passive observers.

The Education Arcade, a learning-game development studio at the Massachusetts Institute of Technology, creates content-centric games for the classroom. *Poikilia*, for example, teaches additive and subtractive color theory. Players need to make their way through a series of dark mazes, carrying torches of red, green, or blue flames (Figure 12.10). Some doors will open only when the player's torches combine to create a particular color. Players can add color by passing through colored flames, or subtract color by passing through colored filters. This mechanic makes for some complex puzzles, where players must plan ahead and consider the primary and secondary colors that will result from a chain of moves. The gameplay in

Poikilia is focused on solving puzzles, but players cannot succeed without building a nimble understanding of color theory. Mastering the science concepts makes solving the problems easier, creating a motivation to engage with the subject matter.

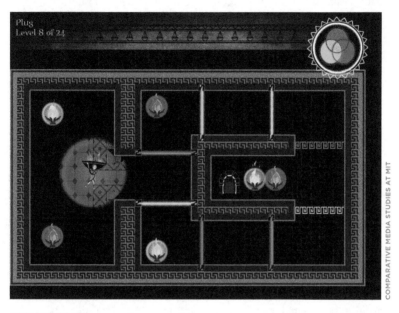

FIGURE 12.10

This puzzle from *Poikilia* cannot be completed without applying a basic understanding of color theory.

Scot Osterweil, the creative director at The Education Arcade, argues that games can be broadly used to impart educational content, saying, "There is play inherent in any subject worth studying."[7] In creating such games, UX designers should bear the following best practices in mind.

Remember That It's a Game

If a game expresses too much of its content through exposition, its flow can get bogged down and it can stop feeling like a game experience. Try to convey as much as possible through gameplay and action rather than dry instruction. If you want to teach chemistry students how reactive elements behave when they're combined, give them some reactive elements to try mixing. Always keep the game moving, and hold the quality of the player experience paramount. Ideally, learners will be self-motivated to seek out more information to make themselves more competent with the game.

---

7 Phone interview with the author, August 16, 2011.

Specialize

A content-oriented game works better as a teaching instrument when its structure is specific to the content. Lessons about nuclear energy should place the player inside a nuclear power plant. Generic formats like quiz games won't take best advantage of the unique strengths of games.

Factor Duration into the Design

Consider what would be an appropriate amount of time to ask players to commit to the game, taking into account the number of learning objectives that it covers. The game should occupy about the same amount of time that would be dedicated to the same subject in classroom instruction. Games that are narrower in focus and cover less subject matter should be relatively brief experiences, whereas more expansive games can reasonably ask for more time.

To Introduce a New Mind-Set

A very different approach to learning games makes use of the cognitive demands a game can place on its players to introduce new ways of thinking about the world. In this case, the learning experience might not be about the acquisition of any specific knowledge at all, but about adopting different models of understanding.

The commercial video game *Portal 2* is a great example of a game that requires players to think in extremely unconventional ways. In it, players have the ability to link two spatially disconnected surfaces by placing one side of a hole on each surface. If you put one side of the hole in the ceiling and the other side of the hole on the floor, and then jump down through the floor, you immediately reenter through the ceiling. It's not real science, but it is a compelling thought experiment, and most other laws of physics are represented faithfully. For example, if the exiting end of the portal were instead placed on a wall, jumping down through the floor would preserve the effect of gravity as you came flying out of the wall.

As *Portal 2* progresses, players must demonstrate increasingly sophisticated levels of facility with the concept as they explore how such a hypothetical technology would pervert the physics of everyday experience (Figure 12.11). At one point, players experiment with directing a laser beam through several targets at once using the portals and a prism. Players need to carefully consider the effect each element will have on the angle of the beam, and make doubly sure they don't inadvertently turn the laser on themselves. This is a cognitively taxing task that requires players to have a fairly nimble command of the laws of physics, while inviting them to reflect more deeply on those laws.

The adventure game *Riven* also introduces new ways of thinking to its players. In particular, players need to investigate the culture of the isolated inhabitants of a chain of islands—a task that invites them to think like sociologists and anthropologists. Players must pull together clues from cave drawings, architecture, technology, temples, and schoolhouses to piece together the story (Figure 12.12). Although they aren't learning about a real people, they are acquiring methods of investigation that can be used in the real world.

Designers who want to create a game to introduce a new mind-set can benefit by observing the following best practices.

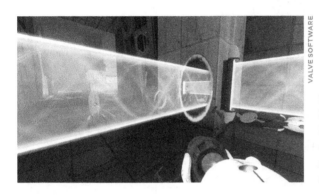

FIGURE 12.11
In *Portal 2*, players learn to think not only outside of the box, but outside of the entire space-time continuum.

FIGURE 12.12
Coming to understand the culture, religion, and way of life of a hypothetical people in *Riven*.

Require Transformation

Make it impossible for players to succeed in the game without having adopted a new way of thinking. In *Riven*, for example, examination of the culture leads to critical insights, without which players would be unable to solve multiple puzzles and advance the story line. Each puzzle is designed to have so many possible combinations that players could not practically solve them by other means. If players are able to guess their way through or succeed by means of simple repetition, the game would fall short on its capacity to introduce new ways of thinking.

Tough Is Good

Both of the games just described—*Portal 2* and *Riven*—become extremely challenging in their later levels, demanding more sophisticated manipulation of the concepts that the player has acquired. That progression is great because it multiplies the benefit of the learning and moves players toward a more dramatic transformation. Of course, earlier levels are also easier, giving the player sufficient practice with the basic ideas to handle the more difficult challenges.

Usability Is Really Good

It's important that if players fail, they fail for the right reasons. If the reason is that they didn't master the concepts, that's legitimate. But if they fail because the way the concepts were presented was fundamentally unclear, then the fault lies with the designer. *Portal 2*'s designers were very careful to ensure that the player can focus on the game's central learning challenge, and they provide multiple cues whenever needed to clarify how game elements that are not central to that objective work. Buttons have simple drawings next to them indicating what they do, and brightly colored dotted lines link the buttons to the things they affect. Removing those elements would make the game harder to complete for all the wrong reasons.

To Guide Experiential Learning

Some of the most innovative uses of educational games are being developed to complement and guide the learner's experience of real-world locations. A team at the University of Wisconsin–Madison created an editor for the iPhone called ARIS, which has allowed for a proliferation of such applications.

One example is Jim Mathews' *Dow Day*, a game that steps players through the events of a 1967 riot in Madison that emerged from protests against Dow Chemical's production of materials used in the Vietnam War. Players walk to the actual locations where the events unfolded, using their iPhones as a guide. Along the way, they meet virtual characters, including a student, a protester, and the dean of the university, who provide historical context and assign them new quests. Importantly, these elements cannot be triggered unless the player gets to the right GPS coordinates, binding the gameplay to the physical space. A highlight of the game comes when the player reaches the top of Bascom Hill, which unlocks an archival film that was shot from the location where the player is standing and shows rioters advancing up the hill (Figure 12.13). This combination of present-day settings, historical context, and game mechanics provides a uniquely tangible way to learn the city's history.

FIGURE 12.13
Like a magic window into the past, *Dow Day* lets players unlock film footage taken in 1967 that was shot from the exact location where they're standing.

Our Minnesota, currently under development by Seann Dikkers, is a quest-based game inside the Minnesota History Center museum that uses a narrative mechanic inspired by games like *World of Warcraft*. Players initiate a tour of mining history in the state by using an iPhone to scan a QR code on a poster of a fictional foreman named Matti the Miner, who directs them down into a mine exhibit (Figure 12.14). Once they reach that location, they encounter a group of virtual miners who point out an ore sample in the real exhibit and ask the player to take it back to the surface (by scanning its code). The game is designed to do things that are difficult to achieve in museums, such as bringing attention to specific objects inside glass cases. Through quests, minigames, and physical interactives, the game also illustrates the process by which mining industrialized the state.

FIGURE 12.14
Our Minnesota transforms the museum experience into a virtual adventure, where players traverse the state and interact with characters integrated into the exhibit.

Best practices for the design of these kinds of experiential learning games are not entirely clear, because they're still very new. Still, some guidelines are emerging from the early work under way.

Get off the Beaten Path

Experiential guides can bring attention to things that would ordinarily go unnoticed by assigning a new significance to them. The places that naturally garner the most attention don't need added incentives to attract visitors. Games can bring people to wonderful smaller locations the way a personal tour from a local native could.

Create an Adventure

A real strength of the game format in experiential learning is its ability to apply a narrative overlay to a location. Assigning players quests can make a location come alive and bring a sense of mission to the experience. For example, *Our Minnesota* culminates in a mine collapse and the rescue of trapped miners.

Work with the Space

The physical location will have a direct effect on the player experience and must be treated as a factor of the design. The traditional snaking paths of museum exhibits might not work as well as an open space that allows movement between different locations, and outdoor tours could potentially route people through real hazards or across unrealistic distances. Walk the tour yourself and test it thoroughly under safe conditions before releasing it to its intended players.

To Develop Skills

Video games very often require players to perform a set of actions over and over again, concentrating attention on the development of specific skills. Players cannot succeed in a game without mastering those underlying competencies. A simple example is the pervasive *Minesweeper*, which started appearing on PCs just when computer mice became commonplace (Figure 12.15). Many people learned basic mouse skills by playing *Minesweeper*, which acclimated players to Windows conventions for visual affordances of clickable objects and to the maxim that left-clicking selects (uncovers a space) and right-clicking modifies (places a flag).

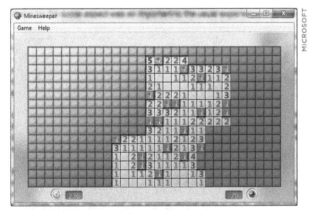

MICROSOFT

FIGURE 12.15
Good old *Minesweeper* gives computer novices practice with a basic set of mouse skills.

Project Injini provides a much more sophisticated example. The visually compelling collection of *Injini* video games for the iPad is designed to build a broad set of essential skills among young children that have cognitive and sensorimotor disabilities ranging from autism to cerebral palsy. It targets children under age five, who are still in critical periods of brain development, and it works to bolster basic aptitudes while the window for improved outcomes is still open.

Injini Frog has players trace out curves from a frog's mouth to dragonflies and beetles that appear around it (Figure 12.16). Then the frog's tongue squiggles out along the same path to catch the bug. Apart from developing fine motor skills and reinforcing cause-and-effect relationships, the frog game is intended to build prewriting skills by encouraging children to practice scribbling and make shapes that can later develop into legible letters.

Injini games are designed to help children advance gradually. *Injini Puzzle* starts by asking the player to fit just one puzzle piece into a blank space (Figure 12.17), ultimately working up to nine-piece jigsaws (Figure 12.18). Before moving up a level, players must complete a puzzle three times in a row without any errors. This requirement ensures that they've mastered the skills they need to be successful in the next level. In this way, games can provide great one-on-one attention that wouldn't be possible in noninteractive media.

Games can support the development of a broad variety of skills by providing structure and motivation to practice. Learning to play the piano or speak French requires repetition and concentration, which can be difficult for people to sustain. Games can put practice into a different context, making it rational and exciting.

Keep in mind the following best practices when designing games to develop skills.

FIGURE 12.16
Injini Frog starts by requiring players to trace simple lines, and then builds to more complex squiggles.

FIGURE 12.17
Players start *Injini Puzzle* by fitting just one piece into a puzzle.

FIGURE 12.18
As their skills develop, players move on to gradually more complex puzzles.

PROJECT INJINI/NCSOFT

Be Forgiving

Players who are having difficulty acquiring a skill are at risk of becoming discouraged. Above all else, you want to keep people in the experience. Avoid game mechanics that are too punitive and that make players feel they cannot recover. When players do make mistakes, make it easy for them to try again. Provide positive encouragement in the game to help them keep at it.

Step It Up

Games can ensure that players progress only after reaching a sufficient level of mastery. The newly acquired skills then prepare players to take on the next level of challenge. This kind of structure supports the development of progressively more sophisticated skill sets.

Mix It Up

Reinforcement requires repetition, but people can become bored with performing the same actions again and again. Variety within the game is important, so allow players to switch among multiple modes of play. It's also beneficial for players to have practice time outside of the game to keep the experience fresh.

To Foster Collective Intelligence

Methods of teaching are adapting in response to the profound changes that the Internet has brought to the ways that people acquire and share information. Skilled users can find reliable information much more efficiently than was ever possible in the past. Groups working in collaboration online can produce more complete answers to questions than any individual person could. This new model for human understanding has been called "collective intelligence,"[8] and game design is well suited to creating experiences that foster it in learning communities. *Yahoo! Answers*, discussed in the previous chapter, is a simple example.

One of the most ambitious experiments in using games to build collective intelligence was *I Love Bees*, created to promote the 2004 release of *Halo 2* for the Xbox. The game started as a URL embedded in trailers for *Halo 2*, leading players to a beekeeping website that appeared to have been hacked and now only displayed cryptic code (Figure 12.19).

---

8   Lévy, P. (1997). *Collective intelligence: Mankind's emerging world in cyberspace.* Cambridge, MA: Perseus Books, pp. 13–18.

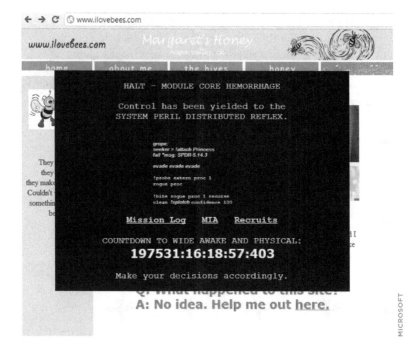

FIGURE 12.19

In *I Love Bees*, a visit to the hacked website www.iLoveBees.com is the player's first step on a grand intergalactic adventure.

The objective was for players to decipher the code and uncover a backstory set in the *Halo* universe, although this goal was never stated in any explicit way. Collaborating in online discussion groups, people advanced competing theories for what the coded messages meant. They eventually hit upon a common connection: GPS coordinates for public telephones around the world, and dates and times at which calls would be placed to each one. People who went to those locations to receive the calls would each receive one portion of the backstory, and again players had to work together online to assemble the complete narrative.[9]

Though the end product of *I Love Bees* was a work of fiction with commercial purposes, the players exercised collective-intelligence aptitudes that are unique to the way the world works today and can be applied to different forms of learning. Quest to Learn, a public charter school in New York City that includes game design in its curriculum, makes use of similar challenges

9 McGonigal, J. (2007). Why *I Love Bees*: A case study in collective intelligence gaming. In K. Salen (Ed.), *The ecology of games: Connecting youth, games, and learning* (pp. 199–228). Cambridge, MA: MIT Press.

on a smaller scale. In one game, biology students received a message from a scientist who had been shrunk to microscopic size and inserted into a human body. Using his observations, students needed to conduct independent research and collaborate to determine where he was located.[10]

Games designed to foster collective intelligence teach something beyond the immediate subject matter. They give people practice in finding information resources and evaluating the reliability of those resources, and in working with teams to find answers to complex problems.

Designers who want to use games to foster collective intelligence should keep a few best practices in mind.

Force Collective Action

So that players have to depend on one another's contributions, no individual should be able to solve the problem alone. Either there's too much work for one person, or no single individual has access to all of the information, as with the telephone messages in *I Love Bees*.

Pool Individual Strengths

One of the great advantages of collective-intelligence exercises is that they can be very inclusive. Different people have different aptitudes, and collective intelligence relies on each person using his or her individual strengths. Your game should demand that players draw on broadly different areas of expertise.

Use Mystery

A persistent theme in games aimed at promoting collective intelligence is the uncovering of a hidden truth. Narratives that culminate in a revelation offer players the sense of an objective they're all working toward, drive interest in the exercise, and promote a feeling of accomplishment at its conclusion.

Playing Smarter

Learning games are evolving into a group of highly diverse, sophisticated, and compelling applications. A substantial community of designers, educators, and researchers has emerged to advance a discipline that has the potential to significantly change the way we approach education. As the world becomes more technologically oriented, video games may play an important role in ensuring the competitiveness of students, workers, and nations.

---

10 Salen, K. (2011, June). *What is the work of play?* Presentation at Games+Learning+Society Conference in Madison, WI.

Games for Persuasion

G ames for action ask people to adopt specific behaviors. Games for learning are designed to teach players something about the world. But persuasive games go a step further than either of these and try to convince people that they should adopt a different point of view. There's an unavoidable overlap among these three—the intended result of persuasion is often some action, and persuasion will always involve some degree of education—but persuasive games are distinct in that they are designed with the intent to effect meaningful change in players' beliefs.

I'm guessing that, for many readers, the idea that games should be used as instruments of persuasion will be the most challenging assertion that I make in this book. Are games really suited to the job of influencing people to vote for a particular candidate, eat healthier foods, or use public transportation? Isn't persuasion serious business?

Games have the ability to command high levels of engagement, and the best opportunities to get a message across come when people are really paying close attention. If UX designers close themselves off to the possibility of using games to persuade, we might miss the chance to get a message across at the very time when people would be most receptive to it.

But even if the opportunity is there, do games really have the potential to capitalize on it? This chapter will describe why, because of their unique qualities, games may actually be an *ideal* way to persuade.

This Is Not a New Idea

The notion of persuasive games actually isn't new at all. Game makers have long recognized that their products could serve as powerful instruments of persuasion.

Historical Precedent

In the 19th century, many games were designed to promote moral messages. Some of these titles remain familiar today.

The first game that Milton Bradley (the man himself) ever published was intended to teach children the connections between life choices and their consequences (Figure 13.1). In The Checkered Game of Life, players move around a board and encounter virtues such as honesty, industry, and bravery, as well as vices such as gambling, intemperance, and idleness. These in turn move the player either to positive life outcomes such as happiness, honor, and wealth, or to ruin, disgrace, and suicide (children's games could be a bit grim in 1860). The modern-day Game of Life has changed substantially but retains some traits of the original, such as the spinner used in place of dice, which at the time were associated with the vice of gambling.[1]

---

1 Lepore, J. (2007, May 21). The meaning of life. *New Yorker*, p. 38.

Similar games popular in the 19th century, such as The Mansion of Happiness (Figure 13.2), promoted Christian moral values; other titles, such as the Game of the District Messenger Boy, advanced capitalist ideals.

FIGURE 13.1
The Checkered
Game of Life carried
a message about
the merits of a
virtuous life.

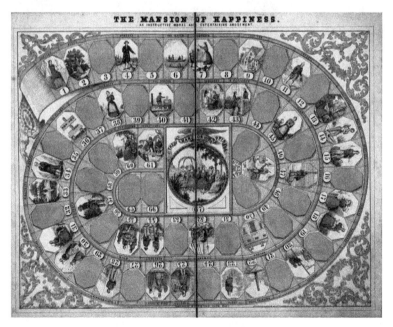

FIGURE 13.2
The Mansion of Happiness, published in 1843, was subtitled
"An Instructive Moral and Entertaining Amusement."

Games for Change

More recently, growing attention has been paid to how video games can make a positive difference in the world. The annual Games for Change conference hosts a festival of games intended to help combat a broad variety of social concerns, including poverty, human rights, and global conflict.

Among the games that have been featured at the festival is *PeaceMaker*, which was designed to underscore the complexities of politics in the Middle East (Figure 13.3). Players take on the role of either the Israeli prime minister or the Palestinian president and make decisions in reaction to real events. Each decision prompts reactions from the public on each side, their leaders, and the international community. Meeting your goals while keeping the region from deteriorating into conflict is a key challenge of the game.

FIGURE 13.3

Painting a complex picture of conflict, Asi Burak's *PeaceMaker* was designed to persuade players that simple resolutions don't exist.

Asi Burak, the lead designer, intended *PeaceMaker* to persuade players that peace in the Middle East is possible, if very challenging. In an interview he said, "We wanted to take one of the most serious problems in the world, and show that video games can put it in context for people more successfully than traditional media."[2] By allowing players to assume the role of either

---

2   Phone interview with the author, December 10, 2010.

side, the game encourages them to empathize with the pragmatic difficulties their respective leaders face in trying to effect an equitable resolution.

Developer Incentives

Federal agencies of the US government have also taken notice of game design and begun issuing grants and other incentives to foster the growth of persuasive games with positive social objectives. In 2010, the Apps for Healthy Kids contest, sponsored by the US Department of Agriculture (USDA) and Michelle Obama's "Let's Move!" campaign, challenged game makers to find ways to persuade children to eat healthier. The contest produced 63 unique entries.

Although the persuasive-game sector is tiny in comparison to the entertainment game industry, it has nonetheless emerged as an important subfield and generated serious interest.

Procedural Rhetoric

Game theorist Ian Bogost uses the term "procedural rhetoric" to describe how games influence people. He argues that games are a form of communication and, as with public oratory, written language, and visual media, they can be used to communicate persuasively.[3] But Bogost further argues that the ability of computers to execute rules—what he calls their "procedurality"—makes them unique as a communications medium. In this regard, they are distinct from books, TV, and stone tablets (especially stone tablets), which express their meaning overtly. In a procedural medium, meaning is communicated through participation. It is through the process of interacting with a computer program that people activate and perceive the procedural rhetoric.

There are also noncomputerized ways to express an idea procedurally. In 1999, the Kansas State Board of Education voted to remove the theory of evolution from the state's science standards. Faced with hostility toward teaching evolution overtly in the classroom, high school biology teacher Al Frisby took to teaching it procedurally instead, through a game.

Frisby had his students, acting like predators, hunt through grass to find different-colored toothpicks, and then pick them up using either forks or spoons. Through this game, he persuaded his students that green toothpicks had a higher likelihood of survival than red toothpicks, and that the predator students outfitted with spoons were more likely to be able to catch their prey than those carrying forks. This exercise allowed students to discover the core tenets of natural selection through gameplay. That's procedural rhetoric.[4]

---

3   Bogost, I. (2007). *Persuasive games.* Cambridge, MA: MIT Press, p. 3.

4   Belluck, P. (2000, August 3). Evolution foes dealt a defeat in Kansas vote. *New York Times.*

The Role of Deliberation

Ian Bogost

Starting with Nolan Bushnell's 1971 coin-op *Computer Space*, arcade video games have shared much in common with pinball and slot machines. They accepted coins as payment, and one of their main design goals entailed persuading players to insert (more) coins. In such games, persuasion is accomplished through basic appeals to addiction and reinforcement. This is an interesting and worthwhile area of inquiry that can help game designers understand how to produce experiences that players feel compelled to complete. However, this kind of persuasion is not my primary interest.

Instead, I am interested in video games that make arguments about the way systems work in the material world. These games strive to alter or affect players' opinions outside of the game, not merely to encourage them to continue playing but to motivate actions beyond the game, out in the material world.

In my book *Persuasive Games*, I make an objection to the concept of "persuasive technology," a general approach to using computing to change people's actions. The checkout system at Amazon.com and other Web retailers tunnels a buyer from product to purchase by removing all links from the page. A camera is positioned conspicuously in traffic to deter speeding, and a computer automatically issues violators a fine. When people act because incentives compel them toward particular choices, they cannot be said to be making choices at all. In such cases, the buyer has not been convinced that a product or seller is desirable, nor has the driver been persuaded that speeding on a particular route is dangerous and should be avoided for reasons of public safety.

To be *persuaded*, not just coerced, people must be given the opportunity to deliberate about an action or belief that they have chosen to perform or adopt. In the absence of such deliberation, outcome alone is not sufficient to account for peoples' beliefs or motivations.

But who cares about deliberation if we get the results we want? If achievement-like structures can get kids to brush their teeth or adults to exercise more, why does one's original motivation matter?

Because to thrive, culture requires deliberation and rationale. When we think about what to do in a given situation, we may fall back on actions that come easily or have incentives attached to them. But when we consider which situations are more or less important, we must appeal to a higher order.

Otherwise, we have no basis upon which to judge virtue in the first place. Otherwise, one code of conduct is as good as another, and the best codes become the ones with the most appealing incentives. After all, the very question of which results we ought to strive for is open to debate.

Ian Bogost is professor of digital media at the Georgia Institute of Technology and an award-winning game designer. His most recent book, How to Do Things with Videogames, *is about games as a mature mass medium.*

Meaning in Games

To be effective at persuading people, games must be able to contain and impart meaning to their players. We often don't think about games in this way, but in fact meaning is communicated in every game. Understanding the game's meaning is a part of understanding how to play the game. If play weren't meaningful, we wouldn't be terribly interested in it in the first place.[5] Meaning gives play a purpose and makes procedural rhetoric possible.

But just because games have meaning doesn't necessarily mean they have ambitions to persuade us about anything in particular. In the vast majority of games, the messages communicated through play are simply about the game itself, especially about what you need to do to win. We can find such self-referential messages scattered throughout games that are familiar to all of us.

Monopoly

Parker Brothers' Monopoly is a game rich with meaning, conveying a number of messages to its players. None of these are written in the instruction manual or explicitly stated in any of the game's materials. Instead, they are communicated through the process of playing the game. The game's messages include:

- **Own a lot of a few things and a little of many things.** Players get the best return on their investment by building houses on a small number of properties. However, owning several individual properties from the many other colors on the board keeps other players from obtaining their own monopolies and pursuing the same strategy.

- **Be willing to make big sacrifices to obtain the things you need the most.** It's often worth mortgaging or selling every property you own if it allows you to afford a single property that you need to execute your strategy.

- **Owning all the railroads provides the most reliable source of income.** The railroads are the only properties with four spaces on the board, so opponents are more likely to land on them and pay you rent. You also don't need to build houses on the railroads to yield greater returns. They consistently pay good dividends.

Especially as you become a skilled player, these messages become increasingly apparent as they lead again and again to winning. People playing the game independently of one another will eventually come to the same conclusions, so these are real and consistent communications.

---

5 Salen, K., & Zimmerman, E. (2004). *The rules of play: Game design fundamentals*. Cambridge, MA: MIT Press, p. 462.

In the modern form of the game, these messages are about the Monopoly game itself and not anything broader. That's especially clear in the railroad strategy; you wouldn't take Monopoly's lesson about railroads as sound financial advice, because there's no expectation that it holds true in the real world. The first two messages might happen to be true of other things in life, but if they are, then it's only by coincidence. Today's game of Monopoly has no agenda to sway people's opinions about anything beyond how to win at Monopoly.

The Sims

Few games are designed to resemble real life so much as *The Sims*. Its virtual people eat, sleep, work, play, cry, laugh, fight, and get it on just like the rest of us.

The Sims also communicates abundant messages that, on the surface, sound like plausible life lessons, including:

- All people need to spend the most time doing the things that really make them happy.

- Time spent expanding your life skills pays off.

- People should find mates with whom they share the most compatible personality traits.

- The right material possessions can help people enjoy life more.

- Neglecting others will damage relationships that you've worked hard to develop.

But at the same time, the game isn't meant to effect any real change in the way its players live. *The Sims* comments on the way life *is*, but it has no agenda to suggest how life *should be*. It was designed to entertain us, not to transform us.

Persuasive Messages in Games

The fact that the messages in most games pertain only to the games themselves is a matter of choice. Designers may instead simply choose to make real-world affairs the subjects of their games, and to incorporate into the rules of play an explicit agenda to change how people think about these issues.

The Landlord's Game

Earlier I made the case that the modern game of Monopoly has no agenda to influence its players' thinking or actions. This is true enough of the version of the game sitting in your closet, which Parker Brothers brought to market in 1936. But Monopoly was derived from an earlier title called The Landlord's Game, which was designed for the specific purpose of persuading its players.

Lizzie Magie invented The Landlord's Game around 1903 to demonstrate how rents paid on land generate disproportionate unearned wealth for property owners to the detriment of their tenants (Figure 13.4). She used the game format to promote the (now arcane) theories of economist Henry George, who advocated a single tax on land ownership to replace other forms of taxation.

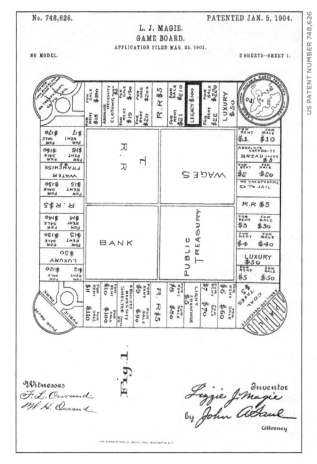

FIGURE 13.4
It's easy to see the modern game of Monopoly in Lizzie Magie's 1904 patent for The Landlord Game, although its persuasive message has been removed.

The ideological mission of The Landlord's Game is laid out plainly in Magie's 1924 patent renewal, where she writes:

> The object of the game is not only to afford amusement to the players, but to illustrate to them how under the present or prevailing system of land tenure, the landlord has an advantage over other enterprises and also how the single tax would discourage land speculation.[6]

This purpose is lost in the commercial version of the game we know today as Monopoly, which modified the rules, objectives, and game board substantially to strip out its original meaning.

The Landlord's Game was in fact a model of a persuasive game: it used the gameplay itself to argue its point, and it was intended to convince people to think differently in the real world. This is the same basic method that UX designers can exploit today to build persuasive games that, in the right applications, can be more effective and compelling than the traditional means of argumentation we might otherwise rely on.

Designing Persuasive Games

How can we best take advantage of the capacity of games to change people's minds? I propose a few guidelines that will help you capture the key characteristics of effective persuasive games.

Define a Core Message

You need to know what you want your game to say, and what you want its players to do or to believe. Examining these questions is the first and most important step toward integrating a persuasive message into your game.

Starting from this point focuses the design so that you can select game elements for their ability to directly support that argument. A well-defined message also helps control the scope of the design by allowing you to recognize digressive game mechanics. These can become a real problem both by muddying the message and by tying up your design and development resources. Dropping problematic elements of the design will allow the game to communicate its core message more efficiently, while keeping your costs down.

Because this step is so important, it's worth making sure you do it the right way. Observe a few best practices when defining your core message.

---

6 US Patent Office. (1924, September 23). *Elizabeth Magie Phillips, of Washington, District of Columbia. Game board.* Google Docs. Retrieved from www.google.com/patents/US1509312?printsec=abstract#v=onepage&q&f=false.

Write It Down

You will need to refer back to the message frequently to keep the design disciplined and to remind yourself of what you want to achieve. If the message isn't written down, it will be easy to forget what you're trying to accomplish and let the design drift. So if your team is going to work in a dedicated space, post the message on the wall so that everyone always knows where it is and can easily refer to it to stay on track.

Be Specific

Author your message using the most precise language available. A vaguely defined message will lead to an uninteresting and unconvincing game experience.

Suppose, for example, that you're designing a game intended to persuade people to invest in mutual funds. If your message is defined as just "Investing money is a good thing," the resulting game mechanic might simply have players adding money to an account that delivers a fixed rate of return. Players will learn little new information about the way the world really works, and they'll have little basis to reflect on their own investment habits.

If instead your message says, "You should invest in mutual funds instead of individual stocks because they can provide reliable returns over the long term without exposing you to too much risk," you can build a much more interesting game with a greater capacity to change people's minds.

Get Everyone's Buy-in

If you're working with a team of designers or creating the game for a client, now is the time to make sure everyone is committed to the approach. Because the game will be built around the precise phrasing of the core message, this is the best opportunity to orient the entire project in the right direction. If significant changes were to be made to the message at a later point, they could require a radical shift in the design or put the entire project at risk. So shop the message with the other people involved in the project, and modify it as needed to gain consensus. If key decision makers hold the purse strings, get them to sign off on the core message.

Be Patient

As tempting as it may be, don't jump too far into the fine details of design until the core message is done. Resisting the urge to flesh out the design can be hard, because you might feel as if you're not moving forward. Often we have a picture in our heads of what the experience will be, and we are enthusiastic about turning it into reality. But there's a real danger of overcommitting yourself to the wrong design by taking off before you know where you're headed. And the process of finalizing the core message really won't take that long. So sit back, chillax, and take satisfaction in the fact that you're starting out on the right foot.

Tie the Message to the Winning Strategy

The competitive dynamic of games drives players to find the most efficient ways to win. If the best strategies that the players can adopt are directly tied to the core message, then players' behavior will tend toward the logical conclusion you want them to draw.

The process of playing the game, then, serves an argument for the truthfulness of its message. Rather than directly asserting that the message is true, a game can require players to adopt the core message as a working hypothesis and use the gameplay to prove to themselves that it's true. To succeed, the players need to buy into the game's point of view. By allowing players to participate in the argument, you can build a more effective rhetoric.

Suppose your game carried a message about fire safety and was meant to convince people to position fire alarms and extinguishers at key places in the home. You would then arrange the dynamics of the game so that buying sufficient home safety equipment and installing it in those particular places resulted in the best possible outcome, whereas worse positioning resulted in progressively poorer outcomes. In executing the game's simulation, winning players would inevitably move toward the ideal installation.

Offer Meaningful Choices

Imagine that a racing game offers players the choice of two cars: a fast one and a slow one. Aside from their speed, the two cars are exactly the same. Which one would you pick? Winning this game would feel distinctly unfulfilling because there are no decisions to weigh. Players would simply pick the unambiguously better car.

Games with these kinds of simplistic choices create no opportunities for players to learn. Ian Bogost writes that for people to be persuaded, they "must have had the opportunity to *deliberate* about an action or belief that they have chosen to perform or adopt."[7] This deliberative process allows people to form a rationale for why they should or shouldn't do something.

To change people's thinking, persuasive games need to give players meaningful choices. It sounds weird, but there has to be some advantage to making the wrong choice, just as there are advantages to the right choice. Suppose that, in the preceding example, the fast car takes greater damage than the slow car. Depending on the number of opportunities the player has to take damage in the game, the slow car could actually be the better choice. This design could become the basis for a game that would promote both the physical safety of cars and more cautious driving habits.

---

7 Bogost, I. (2010, March 3). *Persuasive games: Schell games.* Gamasutra.com.

Keep It Real

One of the greatest persuasive assets of computer games is their capacity to mimic the conditions of the real world. Their "procedurality," to use Bogost's term, allows games to run complex simulations efficiently. Although simulations must always be approximations of reality, they can be sufficiently realistic to give the game's embedded arguments credibility.

For example, a game could easily be built to simulate the environmental effects of invasive species. Real ecosystems are far too complex for any computer to fully replicate, but the essential relationships among a few key plants, animals, and their rough ecological conditions can be demonstrated with enough fidelity for people to accept them as credible.

It's important, however, that the game adhere to reality in every way that really counts, and that it not make unrealistic leaps of logic. If zebra mussels kill sea otters by crowding out their native food source, the game will be believable. If they kill the otters by shooting them with laser blasters, it won't. Mistakes like this sacrifice a key advantage of working in a procedural medium in the first place.

Enable Self-Directed Discovery

Games give designers the opportunity to convince people by allowing players to *discover* things on their own. Discovery is an especially potent way to persuade through games because it gives players a feeling of ownership of the insight they've uncovered. By giving players the space to experiment with many different ways of doing things, you can invite them to think critically about the relative merits of those different choices, and reflect creatively on how things could be done better.

Suppose you want to design a game that promotes a deeper understanding of the advantages and drawbacks of different energy sources. You might run it as a city simulation, in which players need to build a metropolis and construct power plants that can keep pace with the demands of its growing population. To enable self-directed discovery, players may be able to invest in a variety of energy sources—coal, natural gas, solar, wind, hydroelectric, and nuclear. The differentiating attributes of each would include setup costs, maintenance costs, output, reliability, consumption of fossil fuels, and pollution. By experimenting with several different energy sources in the game, players can build an individual assessment of the merits of each.

Case Study: *Fitter Critters*

Fitter Critters, a game created by my team at Megazoid Games for the Apps for Healthy Kids contest, was designed from the ground up to serve as a persuasive game. The contest was intended to produce games that would help solve the problem of childhood obesity by transforming kids' attitudes toward nutrition. This is a very tough nut to crack, because eating habits are deeply rooted in culture. We had to create something that stood as a credible game experience, but that was also persuasive enough to change the choices players make about their diets in the real world.

The Core Message

When we sat down to design *Fitter Critters*, we had a vague sense that we wanted to create a virtual-pet game, but we didn't really know how it should work. We lacked direction, and the design was sputtering and formless. We needed a core message that could serve as the foundation for the game's structure, integrate the contest's objective into the game's design, and get our creative energies flowing.

So we took some time to write down what we wanted the game to say (Figure 13.5), and came up with a two-point message:

- Eating a varied diet rich in vegetables, fruit, and whole grains leads to a better quality of life.

- Eating junk food may have short-term advantages, but in the long run it's not worth the negative health consequences.

MEGAZOID GAMES

FIGURE 13.5
An early paper prototype of *Fitter Critters*. Many elements changed, but the core message (shown here at upper left) remained constant throughout.

Now that we had something to work with, the basic game mechanics quickly snapped into place:

- Players need to shop for their virtual pets' food and feed them on a daily basis.

- A set of scales shows a pet's progress toward daily nutritional needs such as vegetables and whole grains, as well as limits on fats and added sugar (Figure 13.6).

- If players consistently make better nutritional choices, their pets will be healthier.

- Healthy pets will enjoy the benefits of a strong body and lead more prosperous lives.

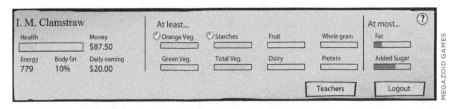

FIGURE 13.6
Every day players need to select foods that will fill all of the green bars (representing positive nutritional attributes) without filling either of their red bars (representing fat and added sugar).

Having a clearly articulated core message also helped us decide which proposed gameplay ideas to drop. For example, one of our early ideas had the game tracking the pet's fullness. Players could feed the pet until its fullness bar reached its maximum, at which point it would reject any more food for a few hours. It seemed like a logical design choice because it would make the game more realistic. But the concept had no rhetorical punch. The fact that you were full had nothing to do with whether you'd eaten healthy food or junk food. You were just full. By dropping fullness, we ended up with a more focused design and saved ourselves valuable development time.

The Winning Strategy

We built a direct relationship between the core message and the ideal strategy that players had to adopt to succeed in the game. If a player's pet is consistently served more nutritious foods, then it will realize a number of positive outcomes:

- **It will make more money at work.** Each day the pet goes off to work while the player isn't using the game. Its earning potential is determined by both its energy level and its overall health, so keeping the critter fitter nets the player more money.

- **It will win more games.** Players can enter their critters into sports competitions (Figure 13.7). The probability of winning and gaining a $50 prize is determined by the critter's health and total body fat.

- **It will get sick less often.** Each day the server decides whether the pet will fall ill, using an algorithm that decreases the likelihood of illness with increasing health. Sick pets can't go to work and can't play sports.

- **It will live large.** Money earned from work and sports prizes can be used not only to buy more food but to decorate the pet's house, introducing collection and customization dynamics into the game.

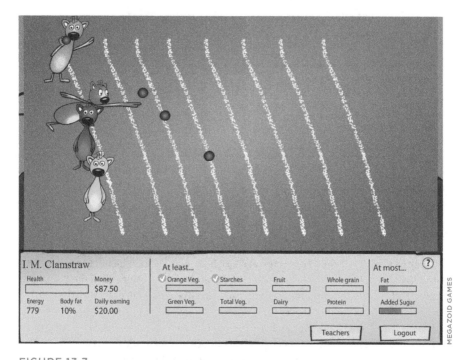

FIGURE 13.7
Players are more likely to win sports competitions if they've been feeding their critter well. Players earn game money for winning, which enables additional rewards.

This design constitutes a laddered reward system, where one type of success leads to another. A lavish pet lifestyle comes from healthier living, and healthier living comes from choices about food—positioning the contest's objective as the inescapable foundation of success. This message is never stated explicitly anywhere in the game, but emerges from the process of playing.

Meaningful Choices

If healthy food offered only benefits and junk food only drawbacks, then the game would present no real choice at all. Players would always pick the healthy food because there would be no reason to consider anything else.

In *Fitter Critters*, there are two built-in advantages to consuming high-calorie foods. First, your pet needs to have a certain minimum level of energy to participate in the sports games. Calorie-rich foods fill up your pet's energy bar quickly, giving it immediate energy. Second, a higher energy level also allows the critter to earn more money from working each day (although this benefit caps at 2,000 calories). That bacon double cheeseburger offers a fast track to higher energy levels.

Of course, unhealthy food choices also have important consequences. Exceeding daily limits on calories, fat, or sugar lowers the critter's health over time. The critter will also develop a taste for junk food and start to reject healthier choices, making it harder to get it back to a healthy lifestyle.

Fitter Critters' design gives players a meaningful choice. It also supports the second part of the game's core message: the short-term advantages of eating junk food are outweighed by the damage done to health and quality of life.

Rooted in Reality

All of the nutrition data for the 675 food items in *Fitter Critters* comes from a data set maintained by the USDA. Moreover, the minimum number of servings the pet needs to meet and its daily limits on fat, sugar, and calories are based on the consumption guidelines set by the USDA for children in the players' age group.

For example, the number of slices of whole wheat bread the player has to feed the pet to fill its whole-grains bar is the same number of slices a child would need to consume on a daily basis in the real world. The amount of healthy foods needed can be surprisingly large, especially for children accustomed to poor eating habits. Managing intake for their pets on a daily basis gives players some sense of the proper proportions of vegetables, whole grains, proteins, dairy, and other foods they should be eating, as well as practice in selecting them.

More broadly, the game's observance of actual food data and nutrition requirements lends its arguments credibility. If eating a single apple magically gave the pet super strength, the game would fail to impart a lesson that players could generalize to their own lives.

Discovery

Fitter Critters creates multiple opportunities for players to learn lessons themselves. One of the key challenges in the game is to use nutrition labels to sift through the multitude of options at the grocery store to discover the foods that will most quickly fill the nutrition requirements while keeping fat and sugar as low as possible. In so doing, players efficiently learn the true nutritional merits and liabilities of different foods. For example, players can discover that sorbets are among the best dessert choices available, since they're free of fat and added sugar and actually provide valuable servings of fruit (Figure 13.8).

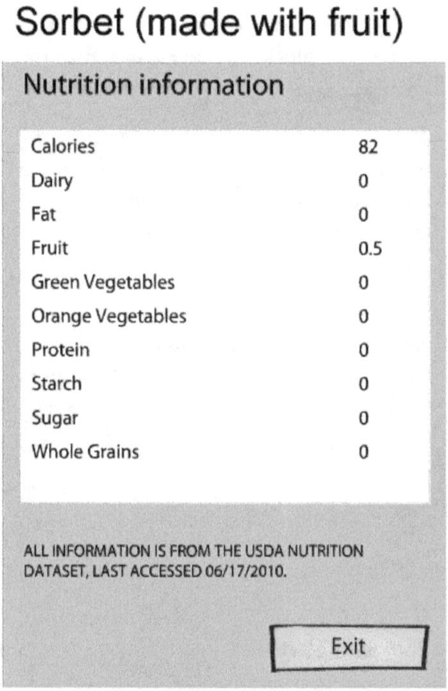

Sorbet (made with fruit)

Nutrition information

Calories	82
Dairy	0
Fat	0
Fruit	0.5
Green Vegetables	0
Orange Vegetables	0
Protein	0
Starch	0
Sugar	0
Whole Grains	0

ALL INFORMATION IS FROM THE USDA NUTRITION DATASET, LAST ACCESSED 06/17/2010.

MEGAZOID GAMES

Exit

FIGURE 13.8
Players need to learn to appraise the nutritional qualities of different foods in order to succeed in the game.

Players also discover the advantages of maintaining a garden and using it as a source of food (Figure 13.9). Harvesting food from the garden allows players to save money for other things (as in real life). Creating an optional resource like this that offers players an advantage if they choose to avail themselves of it is a great way to enable persuasion through discovery.

FIGURE 13.9
Players can discover the benefits of growing a garden to harvest their own fresh vegetables.

Finally, *Fitter Critters* lets players cook meals using the food in their refrigerator. A meal can be sold for up to a 500 percent profit, depending on the healthfulness of its ingredients. Although the reward isn't realistic, it encourages players to think creatively about how nutritious foods could be combined and enjoyed together, while giving tangible value to their combined nutritional attributes.

All of these discovery opportunities were designed to persuade children to think critically about dietary choices and, through their newly gained familiarity with nutrition, apply it in the real world.

Changing Minds

Every medium has been exploited for its rhetorical capacity to persuade its audience. Public oratory, pamphlets, books, radio, TV, film, billboards, bumper stickers, and websites have all served as channels for popular movements, entreaties, political campaigns, and propaganda. Each also offers unique strengths that can be applied to change people's minds.

Games are no different, and UX designers can develop effective persuasive games by playing to the strengths of the format. Through their procedural structure, games are especially adept at demonstrating truths about complex systems and involving people in the process of persuading themselves.

CHAPTER 14

How Games Are Changing

One of the most exciting things about games is that they're constantly evolving. Since the commercial video game market emerged in the 1970s, game designers have competed with one another to invent differentiating experiences and capture greater market share. This continual cycle of innovation has resulted in a broad variety of genres, interaction models, and contexts in which games are played. By looking in the direction that games are moving, UX designers can position themselves to take advantage of the areas of greatest growth in an ever-changing field. And we should expect that many of the innovations emerging in the game sector will also come to impact other user interfaces, since these modes of design are becoming increasingly entangled. In this chapter I discuss five trends that I believe will most strongly influence the direction of game design over the next decade.

Five Trends

1. Mobility

Smartphones and tablets have proven to be surprisingly credible gaming platforms, and they're rapidly changing the way people experience games. They're allowing games to be enjoyed in completely new contexts, at any time and in any place. People carrying mobile devices can play at home, on the commute to work, at work (they're perfect for meetings), at the beach, or while out with friends. Games now follow us wherever we go, opening the possibility of truly ubiquitous experiences. All of a sudden, we have the very exciting ability to lead simultaneous lives in multiple parallel universes.

All this stands in stark contrast to what had become the conventional model for video gaming: sitting passively in a single location in the home and staring at a fixed screen. Life turned off when the game console turned on. Tremendous resources have been invested around this model, building supercomputers for the home that can handle highly sophisticated graphics and sound. With the rise of mobile gaming, though, this model has started to look stodgy and limiting. I don't think it's on the way out, but I do believe that the video game industry establishment is in for a shock as the model declines in popularity. Mobile platforms are rapidly turning into a preferred way of experiencing games because of their combination of high-end technology, unique play contexts, and quality game design.

As physical hardware, mobile devices offer so much for game designers to exploit. Rather than being handicapped by the shortage of hard buttons, joysticks, and mice, mobile games have adapted to take advantage of their more or less standard-issue technology, which comes in no short supply.

Touch Screens

Some mobile games contain literal translations of hardware into soft controls (Figure 14.1). Others focus on new kinds of gameplay that touch screens make possible, such as multitouch and gestural commands (Figure 14.2).

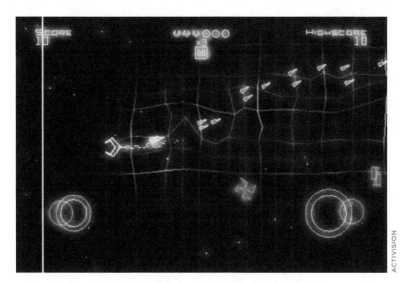

FIGURE 14.1

Players control *Geometry Wars: Touch* by moving their fingers over the two white circles at the bottom of the screen as though they were joysticks.

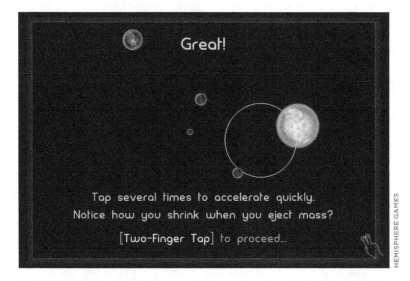

FIGURE 14.2

Osmos allows fluid interaction through gestural commands, taking advantage of the highly accurate multitouch capabilities of modern touch screens.

GPS

Smartphones with GPS capabilities have opened up completely new ways for people to play by allowing games to be continually aware of the player's location. *Geocaching*, for example, invites players to hide objects in public places, and then helps other players hunt the hidden objects down.[1] The ability to overlay game worlds on top of a map of the Earth is a powerful and compelling way to create experiences that push games into real life (Figure 14.3).

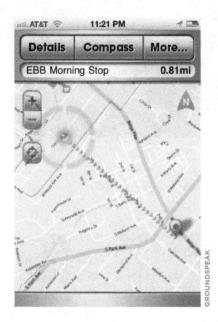

FIGURE 14.3
Hidden treasure lies nearby! *Geocaching* sets players on adventures to find the caches placed by other people.

Cameras

Built-in cameras create many opportunities for creative gameplay. They allow players to incorporate objects from the world around them into the game experience. Games may recognize these objects by bar code, QR code, or image recognition software. Players can import images of themselves and their friends into the game. Cameras open the possibility of creating augmented realities that integrate game graphics with images from real life.

Microphones

One of the most common uses for microphones in gaming has been to facilitate collaboration in cooperative play (or taunting in competitive play). This means of easy communication has also often been an embarrassing problem for games that have no control over what anonymous people in

---

1 Geocaching.com, last accessed February 24, 2012.

adversarial postures say to one another. You should be cautious when creating any game that allows direct communication between people.

Game makers have also experimented with using voice recognition technology as an alternative means of controlling a game. As this technology matures, it will undoubtedly make play more efficient and more engrossing. The guaranteed availability of microphones on every smartphone will inevitably invite experimentation with voice commands.

Accelerometers

Many modern high-end mobile devices come equipped with sensitive accelerometers that can detect changes in the device's motion and orientation in three dimensions. A subgenre of games that make use of these sensors has already emerged in app stores, and it will continue to grow as game makers invent new ways to make use of the technology.

Connectivity

Of course, the overriding reason why people carry smartphones in the first place is that they connect us continually to various networks. This is an enormous advantage for games, which can manage the progression of events from a central server and push updates out to players wherever they are. In addition, a player's access to text and phone services opens the door to alternate reality games that are played over multiple channels while still being governed through a single device. To date, game designers have only scratched the surface of what can be achieved with unbroken mobile connectivity to their players.

2. Social Interaction

Before we had video games, playing a game almost always meant playing with other people. Backgammon, chess, poker, basketball, jacks, and Twister are all valued as much for the social experiences they facilitate as they are for the pleasure of playing the games themselves. Games were traditionally a way of spending meaningful time with other people. The fact that the family of card games designed to be played alone was named "solitaire" speaks to how unusual the solitary game experience was. Spending time playing solitaire could seem a bit pointless (and even a little sad) because the social aspect was so important to the usual experience of games.

Video games changed all that. Although many games had multiplayer components, the usual interaction was between one person and a computer. All of a sudden it wasn't pointless to play alone, because video games can provide meaningful experiences without social interaction. For example, it feels meaningful when you manage to defeat that really tough boss at the end of level 12, even though no other human being might ever know that you did. From a traditional perspective, this is an aberrant way to enjoy games.

The rise of social media in the first decade of the 21st century is bringing games back to their social roots, and people are rediscovering the joy of communing through games. Moreover, social video games are introducing new ways for people to play that simply weren't possible before the technology developed to the point that it has.

Shared Presence

Social video games have given us a way to feel very much in the presence of other people, even though we may not see them or even talk with them. In *Words With Friends*, an online version of Scrabble, players interact almost exclusively by placing words on the board (Figure 14.4). Nonetheless, there's an intimacy to this interaction that feels very much like a dialogue and that bridges both physical and social distances between players. With each move, players are forced to pay attention to each other and to consider how clever, imaginative, and sporting their opponent is. They gain insight into each other's minds, and can sense that their opponent is doing the same.

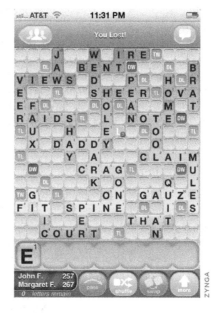

FIGURE 14.4
Words With Friends is not just a game, but a great way to feel connected to other people.

Collaborative Communities

The trend toward playing with strangers online, popularized by massively multiplayer online games, is giving way to playing with people who players already know. Many social video games specifically encourage players to play with as many established friends as they possibly can, often dozens at a time, providing in-game advantages to roping friends in. Amplified by social networks, these games facilitate a kind of hypersocial play that has no real precedent. Of course, encouraging large multiplayer networks is a means of promoting the game. But it also has unique effects on human interaction.

Rather than promoting competition, these games tend to focus on collaborative play in which people help one another out, sending gifts, providing energy, or doing work for one another. By rewarding a cycle of cooperation and reciprocity, they promote positive interactions between people and foster the growth of communities of play that work together. One can imagine that this may point toward a new model for how large groups of people could be motivated to work in concert with one another online, perhaps for work or charity. Political campaigns, which can have a playful spirit, could be revolutionized by building collaborative communities of volunteers and donors through gameplay.

3. Casual Play

Since the mid-1980s, video games have been trending toward longer experiences to justify their cost. Among dedicated gaming communities, greater length of play was generally seen as a mark of their value. A $10 movie ticket may provide 2 hours of entertainment, but a $50 game can provide upwards of 100 hours of gameplay. For people who have the free time, video games can be great buys.

But long games can also be exclusionary of players who can't commit that much time. In *Kingdom Hearts II*, the tutorial alone takes several hours to complete. The complex controls of many games require sustained effort to learn and master. *Tomb Raider III* provided a limited number of opportunities throughout the game when players could save their progress, and they were afforded these opportunities only once every few hours. Such games assume a dedicated player—one who has the ability to sit with a game for long periods, give it 100 percent attention, and stick with it until it's finally over. Even then, some games can be replayed in a different difficulty mode. If there weren't such a substantial market for these kinds of experiences, we might mistake this sort of game design for a kind of hubris.

Recently there has been tremendous growth in casual games, which ask much less of the player and so appeal to a wider range of people with varying amounts of time on their hands. These are games that work for busy professionals, busy parents, busy college students, and even busy kids. A few characteristics are common to all casual games.

Short Learning Curves

Casual games are easy to pick up and play. They're highly usable and demand little expertise with the interface. In fact, the less time it takes to learn a casual game, the more successful it will be, because fewer people will give up on it before they've had a chance to really experience the gameplay. A short learning curve also has the advantage of allowing people to disengage from play for some time, and then pick it back up without losing their expertise. UX designers bring a valuable skill set to casual games because they're practiced in making interfaces more intuitive and learnable.

Short Engagements

Casual games can be enjoyed in short bursts whenever the interest arises. Players can turn them on when they have a spare minute or two, and turn them off at a moment's notice without suffering any losses in the game. All saving is completely automatic and up-to-the-minute, so players don't need to be concerned about seeing a quest through to completion.

Short Completion Times

For casual games that have specific ending conditions (and many don't), it doesn't take dozens or hundreds of hours to bring play to a conclusion. Shorter completion times allow the player to feel the satisfaction of a resolution with less effort.

High Replay Value

To make up for their shorter engagement times, casual games give players reasons to come back again and again. The Tamagotchi virtual pet, for example, involved only a few minutes of interaction at a time, but it required players to engage with it often enough to maintain their pet's health. In this way, casual games trade off a sustained gameplay experience for a low level of recurring engagement.

4. Radical Interfaces

The fierce competition among video game manufacturers has created pressure to differentiate products in any way that can be imagined. Attempts at creating unique experiences spread from innovations within the games themselves to encompass the interfaces through which people play them. This trend is great for UX designers because game makers are actively exploring the feasibility and utility of interfaces that depart radically from conventional setups. By taking on the risk of engineering these unique designs and bringing them to market, game makers are leading research and development that could give UX designers insight into the ways people will be interacting with machines in the future.

Motion Control

Sony introduced the first commercially successful motion control scheme in 2002 for the PlayStation 2; it was a camera that projected the player's image on-screen, with graphics that responded to motion. The EyeToy sold more than 10 million units worldwide[2] and initiated a race among game console manufacturers to invent alternative ways of controlling game experiences. The most recent iterations, the XBox Kinect and PlayStation Move, have driven cutting-edge imaging technologies directly from the laboratory into the home and demonstrated the plausibility of controlling a user experience through physical movement. Motion control allows for a very literal transposition of actions into input. An especially notable feature of games played on these systems is the way the interface just dissolves, leaving a feeling of direct connection between the person and the on-screen events.

In time, the lessons learned from motion-controlled video games will allow the technology to make the leap into other experiences as well. Microsoft is actively encouraging this development by investing seed money into start-ups that use the Kinect hardware in nongaming applications. It's easy to imagine that at some point soon you won't need to hunt for a remote control to pause, rewind, or turn up the volume while you're watching a movie on your motion-controlled TV, because all of those core functions will be supported by simple hand gestures. You'll turn lights, air conditioners, and sound systems on or off by pointing to them. Traffic lights at busy, motion-controlled intersections will reflect the gestures of white-gloved crossing guards. As in each of these cases, motion control will be especially useful when the users are physically separated from the objects they're controlling.

Linked Displays

For years, Nintendo has been exploring the possibilities of combining a main display with subdisplays for different players. The GameCube console, for example, could be connected to multiple Game Boy handheld systems using a cable. This setup allowed players to share one main display on the television, while individual players could keep personal displays on their Game Boy screens hidden from one another. For example, people playing football games could secretly select plays on the Game Boy, and then execute them on the shared screen. *The Legend of Zelda: The Wind Waker* allowed one person to play the primary game on the shared screen while another person played a supporting role giving health and attacking enemies on the Game Boy. Nintendo has made a new commitment to this unique combination of group and individual experiences in its Wii U console, the controllers of which each have their own built-in touch screen displays.

As multiple devices with independent displays make their way into the hands of consumers, it seems inevitable that designers of nongame experiences will explore similar architectures. It's a great model for

---

2   Kim, T. (2008, November 6). *Eye-to-eye: The history of EyeToy.* Gamasutra.com.

collaboration: letting a room full of people contribute simultaneously to a single document projected on-screen from separate programs on their laptops. For example, a Web design team consisting of information architects, designers, content writers, and developers, each working in separate applications on their individual laptops, could see the pages of a site coming together in real time on the projected screen through a linked application, better supporting a shared vision while improving the whole team's productivity.

Experimental Interactions

Game designers have sometimes experimented with radically different ways of interacting, just to see what new kinds of experiences would result. Nintendo invented a format called microgames, found in titles such as *WarioWare: Smooth Moves*, that consists of a large number of individual games, each lasting only seven or eight seconds. Microgames require players to figure out how to control each game on the basis of visual affordances, and to master the game before time runs out. Microgames rely on a system that supports rapid learning of new interfaces based on minimal cues—an experiment that could have great relevance to UX design.

One-button games have become a recent fad at the fringes of game development, eschewing the 18-button controllers of modern consoles to milk all the control they can out of a single input. In games like the oddly compelling *One Button Bob*, the function of the button shifts from one context to another—allowing the player to run, jump, fly, retreat, climb, and attack as needs dictate (Figure 14.5). Such one-button interfaces can be instructive to designers creating controls for people with poor motor coordination and limited mobility. They also lend themselves to the development of more efficient control schemes that may have multiple inputs but allow a great many actions to be initiated from each one.

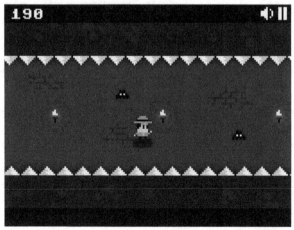

FIGURE 14.5
One Button Bob cleverly demonstrates how lots of different actions can be mapped to a single button. Here the player flies by tapping quickly.

GameShare, a product invented by game researcher Ben Sawyer, splits the functionality of a single game controller so that two people can contribute to a game simultaneously (Figure 14.6). One player is in charge of movement in the game, while the other executes actions using large buttons that can be hit with the hands or feet. The system was intended to help parents and children play together by requiring two participants and by assigning movement tasks, which require finer skill, to one person. We could say that GameShare presents an interesting new way for players to collaborate, but that's sort of missing the point. More saliently, it explores how an interface can be used to build stronger bonds between people.

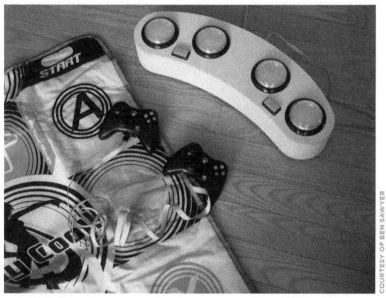

COURTESY OF BEN SAWYER

FIGURE 14.6
GameShare splits a standard game controller into two pieces, allowing players to collaborate on the actions of on-screen characters.

Game designers are opening up new frontiers in interactivity, into which UX designers will inevitably expand. As practitioners, we will do ourselves a great favor by recognizing the relevance of game design to our own field, and staying current with the innovations that video games are introducing into the market.

5. Emotional Engagement

Increasingly, video game designers are seeking ways to engage players emotionally by aspiring to the kinds of experiences we expect more from art, literature, and film. They're turning to narrative elements and the development of characters in whom the players are invited to feel an emotional investment. Games like *Red Dead Redemption*, *Heavy Rain*, and *L.A. Noire* drive this effort through recorded dialogue read by professional actors, interspersing the gameplay with cinematic cutscenes that put the player's progress through the game in a narrative context.

The advanced state of modern technology greatly enhances the emotional resonance that games can achieve. In *Shadow of the Colossus*, the player is given the role of a young man trying to resurrect a woman he loves. Accompanied only by your horse, Agro, you travel a vast landscape searching for hostile giants to vanquish, in return for which a voice from above promises to grant you the woman's life.

An important part of the game's effect is the uncanny realism of the horse's behaviors (Figure 14.7). They're really remarkably perfect. Not only is Agro's visual rendering very convincing, but he moves, whinnies, grazes, plays, and nuzzles as real horses do. He comes faithfully when you whistle, and comes looking for you when you wander out of his sight. You spend long periods traveling the barren landscape together. This realism is a deliberate design decision intended to reproduce the same feeling of an emotional relationship we would develop with a pet or a loved one in the real world. It takes advantage of the systems in the brain that insist such connections be formed, willingly or not. Over time you develop the instinctive sense that Agro is a real, living creature who values your presence. The real proof of the emotional connection you've developed to the game comes near the end, when Agro plummets from a crumbling cliff while trying to reach you. It's an extraordinary moment that's surprisingly difficult to watch.

Shadow of the Colossus explores the emotional effects of relationship building—something to which interactive experiences are especially well suited. Unlike the typical response to literature or film, the game player takes on a personal role within the experience and has some ownership of the relationships established with other characters. As more designers adopt the powerful possibilities latent in video games, we will see new forms of art emerging from the raw material of interactivity.

FIGURE 14.7
Shadow of the Colossus invites players to build an emotional connection to a virtual horse, who serves as a loyal friend in a lonely setting.

Game On

The objective of this book is to predict not the future of the video game industry, but the future of user experience design. Inevitably, games will be a significant part of what UX designers do and of how we define ourselves.

Descending from a common ancestry, video game design and UX design are due for a reunion. New communities of designers have emerged to explore the new possibilities that open up when we stop thinking of our respective disciplines as irreconcilably partitioned forms of design. A new breed of interactive products will acclimate user-players to the feeling of blended experiences in which they not only accomplish something but have fun doing it. To operate successfully in this future, UX designers will need to develop within ourselves the theory, skills, and practices needed to create high-quality player experiences.

Moreover, we will need to embrace a different way of thinking about experience. We've devoted our attention to maximizing the usability, efficiency, learnability, usefulness, and beauty of user interfaces. Embracing game design requires us to go a step further and devote ourselves to people's intrinsic enjoyment of the experiences we design.

Index

A

absolute nonlinearity, 74
accelerometers, on mobile devices, 221
accomplishment, 44
achievements, 140–141
action
  encouraging in games, 67
  incorporating real world into
      gameplay, 148
action/arcade games, 81
action-based game, 54
adults, as players, 53
Adventure for the Atari 2600, 143
adventure games, 62, 81
adventure, in learning games, 190
aesthetics, 32
  playtesting and, 101
affect, playtesting and, 101
agency, learning games and, 172
Age of Empires III, 180, 181
age of players, 52–53
aggression, 43
agility, playtesting and, 101
AI, rules-based, 61
Algebra Touch, 174
alternate existence, creating, 159
alternate reality games, 81
Amazon
  customer ratings, 128
  Gold Box, 166–167
Ambinder, Mike, 52
Angry Birds, 80, 174
Animal Crossing, 78, 135, 141
Apps for Healthy Kids contest, 201
ARIS, 188
The Art of Game Design (Schell), 100
art time, paper prototyping to save, 89
assessment, games for, 178–195
Asteroids, 86
asymmetrical power of players, 80
asynchronous multiplayer games, 77
attributes of game character,
      choices, 178

autonomy, 41–42, 108
avatar, customizing physical
      appearance, 178

B

badges, in Foursquare, 155
balance
  in game elements, 31–33
  paper prototypes and, 87
  playtesting and, 101
  point systems and, 129
baseball, 45, 80
  fantasy teams, 93
Battleship, 79
behaviorism, 112–119
  design of consequences, 115–119
  free will and, 123
  in video games, 119–122
  punishment, 114–115
  reinforcement, 114
      schedules, 117–119
Bejeweled, paper prototype for, 90
blackjack, 59
  conflict, 69
Blizzard, 37
bocce, 71
Bogost, Ian, 201, 208
Bolt, Nate, Remote Research, 102
bookkeeping, for paper prototypes, 93
boundaries of game, 18
Bradley, Milton, 198
Braid, 63
Brain Age, 127, 129
brain games, 81
brainstorming, conflicts, 70
Burak, Asi, 200

C

Call of Duty: Modern Warfare 3, 54
cameras, and gameplay, 220
CardioMiles, 162
casual play trends, 223–224
categories of games, 16

X

XBox Kinect, 225

Y

Yahoo! Answers, 152–153

Z

Zimmerman, Eric, 20
Zynga, 163
  charitable initiatives, 164

ACKNOWLEDGMENTS

I owe enormous thanks to my publisher, Lou Rosenfeld, not only for championing this book but also for the tremendous support he's provided to me over the years. He's been an inspiring force in my life, and his belief in me has made all the difference in who I am today.

A lot of people have generously lent their expertise and viewpoints to this book, and I sincerely hope that I've managed to cite all of them here. Ian Bogost, Jim Gee, Stone Librande, Jamie Madigan, and Jesse Schell not only contributed the sidebars in this book, but were kind enough to give personal guidance and review chapters as they were in progress.

My wonderful editor was JoAnn Simony, and the technical reviewers were Stephen Anderson, Mathias Crawford, and Nathan Verrill. This is a much better book as a result of their careful attention and thoughtful input.

Other people who made critical contributions of time and expertise include Mike Ambinder of Valve Software; Nate Bolt of Bolt|Peters; Luis Von Ahn of Carnegie Mellon; Seth Cooper of Foldit; Dennis Crowley of Foursquare; Scott Rigby of Immersyve; Jason Haas, Eric Klopfer, and Scot Osterweil of MIT's Education Arcade; Anna Johnson and Sooin Lee of Project Injini; Richard Marks and Eric Matthews of Sony Computer Entertainment; and Seann Dikkers and Ben Shapiro from the University of Wisconsin. Additional reviews were provided by Catriona Cornett, Jim Kalbach, Julie Price, and Kyle Soucy. Thank you all so much for your help!

People who made pertinent impacts in my professional life include David Wright, who first provided a platform for me to start designing games; Todd Horning, Rob Patey, and Mike Rosario, with whom I collaborated on those projects; Richard Dalton and Gina Puzo, who pushed me hard to start talking about games; and James "Chip" Chiponis, Andrew Karetas, and Bri Lance, who each made a leap of faith to pursue game projects with me. I sincerely hope that I've lived up to the confidence they've all invested in me.

I would certainly be remiss if I didn't thank my parents, Margie and Charlie, who have made so many sacrifices on my behalf and to whom I can never be sufficiently grateful, and my siblings Steve, Chris, and Cath. You are each, in your own way, a part of this book.

I opened the book with a dedication to my wife Amanda, and I must close with a note of gratitude to her. She's put up with so much over the course of this project, above and beyond what could ever be reasonably asked. I will always be thankful for the support she has given me, not only during this period, but throughout our time together.

—John Ferrara, Philadelphia, April 2012

ABOUT THE AUTHOR

 John Ferrara has worked as a user experience practitioner since 1999 and began designing video games in 2001. His nutrition education game *Fitter Critters* was a top prizewinner in the 2010 Apps for Healthy Kids contest sponsored by Michelle Obama's "Let's Move!" campaign, and it is currently being tested in public elementary schools. In 2011 he co-founded Megazoid Games, which focuses on creating mobile, social, and educational player experiences.

John works as an information architect at Vanguard and has done significant work in the past for Unisys and GE. He holds a BA in Communication Arts from Hofstra University and an MA in Communication Studies from West Chester University. He gets really excited about things like search algorithms, human evolution, artificial intelligence, and independent films of the 1990s. He freely admits that he probably plays too many video games, but swears up and down that he's got it under control and can stop at any time. He lives in the Philadelphia area with his beautiful wife and superhero daughter.

KEEP UP WITH ROSENFELD MEDIA

We'd love to let you know of new book signings, discounts and promotions, author presentations, and other Rosenfeld Media news. There are plenty of ways to stay in touch:

- Subscribe to our free monthly newsletter, the Rosenfeld Review: is.gd/9viTRS
- Visit our site: www.rosenfeldmedia.com
- Subscribe to our RSS feed: feeds.rosenfeldmedia.com/rosenfeldmedia
- Follow us on Twitter: @rosenfeldmedia
- Email us: info@rosenfeldmedia.com